DAMAGE CONTROL

Eric Dezenhall is the CEO of Dezenhall Resources in Washington, D.C. He began his career in the White House Office of Communications during the Reagan presidency. Prior to starting his own firm, he worked at an international public relations agency and a political consulting firm. He is also the author of *Nail 'Em: Confronting High-Profile Attacks on Celebrities and Businesses.* His forthcoming novel *The Devil Himself* will be published by Thomas Dunne/St. Martin's in the summer of 2011

John Weber is the president of Dezenhall Resources and the firm's second partner. He oversees client services and is the primary liaison with its affiliate agencies in the United States and Europe. Weber previously served as a senior manager at three of the world's largest public relations firms. He began his career in marketing and advertising.

Visit their Website at www.DezenhallResources.com

D0967576

DAMAGE CONTROL

The Essential Lessons of Crisis Management

Eric Dezenhall and John Weber

PROSPECTA PRESS

First published in the United States of America by Portfolio, a member of the
Penguin Group (USA) Inc. 2007 and reprinted in paperback by Portfolio, 2008.

978-1-935212-24-9 paperback
978-1-935212-25-6 ebook

THIS NEW REVISED PAPERBACK EDITION IS PUBLISHED BY
PROSPECTA PRESS, AN IMPRINT OF EASTON STUDIO PRESS, LLC
P.O Box 3131
Westport, CT 06880
203-454-4454
www.prospectapress.com

Quote from *Jaws*. © 1975 Universal Pictures, Courtesy of Universal Studios Licensing, LLLP.
Quote from *National Lampoon's Animal House*. © 1978 Universal City Studios, Inc. Courtesy
of Universal Studios Licensing, LLLP.
Quote by P.J. O'Rourke. By permission of the author.

June 2011
Manufactured in the United States of America

To Donna and Stephanie

ACKNOWLEDGMENTS

The authors wish to thank the following people for their behind-the-scenes assistance with *Damage Control*: Bernadette Malone, Adrian Zackheim, Will Weisser, Kris Dahl, Bob Stein, Susan Haralson, Stuart Dezenhall, and Malinda Waughtal.

AUTHORS' NOTE

This book includes numerous case histories and examples of both well and poorly managed crises. While some of these are based on our direct involvement, many are not. Where an example is based on our experiences, we have obscured the facts to protect the identities of clients we did not want to reveal. It has always been, and will continue to be, the corporate policy of Dezenhall Resources not to reveal our clients or to discuss, without their permission, our work on their behalf.

CONTENTS

INTRODUCTION

You're gonna need a bigger boat.

—CHIEF BRODY, *JAWS*

We knew we weren't going to take the case within thirty seconds of walking into the boardroom. This prospective client—a large consumer health products concern under attack by the news media, government regulators, activist groups, trial lawyers, and shareholders—was going to get slaughtered, but not because its crisis was so bad. It wasn't as if its best-selling product was alleged to be killing people.

The prospective client—let's call the company Socrates—called us in to meet its crisis management team. We had been under the impression that the objective of the meeting was to listen to Socrates tell us its side of the story—why its best-selling product was under attack. Then, presumably, we'd give Socrates our initial ideas on how to defuse the attack.

One look at the dynamics of the room, however, and we knew we had landed smack dab in the middle of what we sarcastically call a "beauty contest." Beauty contests are presentations that are held ostensibly to hear out the ideas and credentials of the potential consultants available for hire. Sounds legitimate, right? The real purpose, however, of a beauty contest in many high-stakes PR assignments is to identify the consultant who is least likely to get anyone sitting at the table fired.

A company in crisis is often no longer a company at all: It's a collection of individuals, each of whom is looking for personal cover. Truth be told, the company's welfare was low on the priority list of the individuals in this room.

This probably seems like a cynical assessment.

Welcome to the blunt talk of contemporary damage control, which requires a sober appreciation of both human nature and the tides of Fortune. After all, crisis management is storytelling, and a good story begins by recognizing the omens set out for us by the flawed human beings and institutions in the narrative. When *Jaws's* Chief Brody observed that Quint's crew needed a bigger boat, he was doing more than making an observation; he was making a strategic assessment of both the practical tools that would be needed to catch the great shark and inquiring about the resolve of the shark-hunting team.

Resolve must be anchored in a realistic appreciation of the challenges at hand. Ironically, in an age of crisis, business culture is living in a "Spintopia"—an environment in which business schools, consultants, and pundits dispense Mother Goose aphorisms about crisis management that contradict what real-world life experience teaches. The advice crisis consultants give is often designed to benefit the consultant, not the client.

We're in the crisis management business. A crisis manager's

job is to make bad news go away. We are the trauma surgeons of public relations. Corporate scandals, high-profile litigation, product safety allegations and recalls, boycotts, brand smears, government investigations and prosecutions—these unwanted events are our daily challenges.

Conventional public relations is enamored with "reputation management," "empowerment," "trust," "the message," and other guru-driven happy talk that serves little purpose other than to give people in very tough situations the illusion of control.

"Martha Stewart just needs to apologize," a pundit says on CNN. "If Nixon had just said right away, 'I screwed up,' there would have been no Watergate scandal," a political science professor speculates. "If Coca-Cola had just recalled their product right away, that whole Belgian mess wouldn't have happened," a business school case-study lecturer asserts. "We've got to tell 'em all the *good things* your products do," a public relations account executive assures her polluting client in a new-business pitch, adding with a sparkle, "Remember, a crisis is an opportunity to get your message out!"

Crisis management is the enterprise of telling ugly truths. Ideally, it is the pursuit of redemption in the marketplace. When one has done wrong, repentance is required. When one has been wronged, a vigorous defense must be mounted.

Even before the meeting at Socrates formally began, our team, drawing on eighty collective years in the high-stakes communications business, saw four telltale signs of crisis management doom:

1. **The chief executive officer was absent.**

   The task of crisis and issues management had fallen to Socrates'
   public relations chief. There's no question that the chief communications officer must play a key role in the crisis, but, as a
   rule, companies that see communications as the answer to its
   problems rarely have the management juice to make the decisions necessary to resolve the crisis. Does the PR chief have the
   authority to recall a product? Can she order a product reformulation? Can she shut down—and then reboot—worldwide
   production and distribution? Does she have the ear of Wall
   Street analysts? Does she have bet-the-company authority? The
   answer to all these questions is probably no.

   In times of crisis, the chief executive officer must be the
   chief crisis officer, or, if not the CEO, the business unit chief
   who has the authority to make fundamental decisions. In
   the gathering at Socrates, the real powers to resolve the crisis
   were not in the room.

2. **There were too many people at the meeting.**

   The boardroom was filled. There were more than twenty
   people gathered from every discipline within the company,
   not to mention other outside consultants. Many of them
   were primed to take notes on laptops. The group leader was
   very pleased that she was seeking "input" from Socrates'
   "diverse knowledge partners." The corporate-speak was suf-
   focating and betrayed the true purpose of the meeting: making the participants feel comfortable with the process.

Effective crisis management teams are small. While they may indeed collect input from a variety of sources, they are not meant to be New Age esteem-building entities where everybody has a voice and gets to feel special. That so many of Socrates' players were ready to memorialize the meeting's proceedings on their laptops was a blaring warning sign. It's a safe bet that these jottings would wind up in court or on the front page of the *Wall Street Journal.*

3. **Someone mentioned the "Tylenol case."**

One of the more hackneyed features of most introductory crisis management meetings is the obligatory citation of the famed 1982 Tylenol case in which seven people died as a result of cyanide poisoning from tainted Tylenol capsules. The brand famously recovered after a product recall and introduction of tamper-resistant packaging. Our ill-fated meeting with Socrates was to be no exception. A Power-Point image on the screen referenced the Tylenol case, and an exuberant midlevel employee was poised to present an argument for capitulation.

While there are many admirable features of the Tylenol case (which will be explored in depth later), its invocation has become a mantra for managers desperate for a guaranteed happy ending. In reality, the Socrates crisis has little in common with the Tylenol case.

4. **Someone recommended more research, a plan, and the formation of a committee.**

    There's a myth that the biggest threat to sound crisis management is panic. Actually, it's quite the opposite: The biggest threat is the instinctive corporate desire to do nothing when facing danger. "Doing nothing" can never be openly presented as a viable option, of course. So, it is introduced with the thoughtful observation that "we shouldn't run off half-cocked" and then followed by a series of memos, plans, presentations, and the like that make people feel busy but do little to calm the raging seas of pending disaster.

    Here's the dirty little secret of the procrastinators: It is not so much that they oppose action per se; it's that they neither know what to do nor have any tolerance for risk of any type. Memo anyone?

In the crisis management business, we don't turn away work on the grounds that a case appears to be difficult—a crisis by nature is supposed to be hard. Nevertheless, we cannot help save an enterprise that does not want to be saved. We didn't sign on with Socrates because we felt the company was constitutionally incapable of resolving its crisis.

Our business by its very nature is intimate, and we take on a limited number of cases, preferably those for which we can make an impact. "Impact," of course, doesn't necessarily mean victory, but it does mean there is more likely to be a correlation between input and results.

Crisis management, while a rare corporate discipline, is nevertheless a fundamental one because the future of the enterprise is on the line. A grieving widower appeared on *Larry King Live* in 1992 and speculated that his wife's terminal cancer was caused by a cellular telephone: Motorola, the leading cell phone manufacturer, saw its stock drop by 20 percent in the following days. Merck's recall of its arthritis drug Vioxx cost the company roughly $750 million in the fourth quarter of 2005 alone; a Merrill Lynch stock analyst estimated that damages against the company could run between $4 billion and $18 billion. Perrier was toppled from its perch atop the best-selling bottled water mountaintop after the chemical benzene was found in its product. And when the Audi 5000 was accused of "sudden acceleration," its sales evaporated and the Audi brand essentially vanished from the U.S. market for a decade.

WHO SURVIVES?

Damage Control examines these survival factors in greater detail later; however, our encounter with Socrates strongly suggested that this company didn't have what it takes to weather the hurricane it was facing. Companies (and individuals) that survive crises tend to have certain features in common, features that are often evident in the first moments of an engagement:

- *They have strong leaders* who have broad authority to make decisions.
- *They question conventional PR wisdom* and do not worship at the altar of feel-good gurus who espouse "reputation management," the canard that corporate redemption follows popularity.
- *They are flexible,* changing course when the operating climate shifts (which it usually does).

- *They commit significant resources* to the resolution of a crisis with absolutely no guarantee that these resources will provide results.
- *They have a high threshold for pain,* recognizing that things may get worse before they get better.
- *They think in terms of baby steps, not grandiose gestures,* which explains Rome's success, after all.
- *They know themselves,* and are honest about what kinds of actions their culture can—and cannot—sustain.
- *They believe that corporate defense is an exercise in moral authority,* and that their critics are not necessarily virtuous simply because they purport to be standing up for the "little guy."
- *They are lucky,* often catching unexpected breaks delivered by God, Nature, Fortune, or some other independent factor.

Enterprises and individuals under siege need all the help they can get these days. Since the tech bubble burst and corporate scandals have come to fill the media vacuum once occupied by lionizing messianic CEOs, it seems as if no one's exempt from hostile scrutiny.

Crises are now judged not only by financial (Did the company recover?) and ethical (Was the public welfare served?) standards, but by whether the company handled its crisis effectively in the eyes of Wall Street, Madison Avenue, the plaintiff's bar, and twenty-four-hour-a-day cable news. Inevitably, the airwaves are filled with experts from various fields who will opine that the crisis is being mismanaged. (Saying "all's well" doesn't make for very good TV.) The focus of the postcatalyst debate will be on the public relations aspects of the crisis, with a grotesque overestimation of what deft PR can accomplish and a disregard for the operational, legal, political, and contextual nuances.

REAL DAMAGE CONTROL

The term "damage control" originated when the Navy had to grapple with a new technology—the torpedo—and its devastating impact on a vessel. Even if torpedoed, a vessel could sometimes recover and carry out its mission *if* the crew had the right skill set. Only in the recent media age has the term been applied to public relations and vulcanized to imply that a slick trick can undo the destruction of a metaphorical torpedo's impact.

Wal-Mart, once the very symbol of heartland American success, is routinely framed as a cultural villain in the popular press. The once venerable Arthur Andersen accounting firm imploded in an ethics scandal and was vindicated only *after* declaring bankruptcy. The "blockbuster" drugs Vioxx and Celebrex were respectively recalled and fettered by terrifying safety claims. Dan Rather, the "Voice of God" of network television news for decades, was deposed in a scandal involving flawed sources and forged documents. The venerable Hewlett-Packard was rocked by a seemingly idiotic corporate spying scandal. Nothing escapes a torpedo.

Meanwhile, for every company that is vilified for mismanaging its affairs, another one resolves its problems with little fanfare: Tyco, which focused on internal audiences such as its customers, comes to mind, as does General Electric's smooth transition between legendary chief Jack Welch and his successor, Jeff Immelt. For every conviction for corporate fraud (WorldCom's Bernard Ebbers), there is a stunning acquittal

(HealthSouth's Richard Scrushy). What accounts for these different outcomes?

How was the same Martha Stewart who was shredded in the press for her clumsy handling of the public relations surrounding her criminal case eventually hailed as a genius upon her release from prison? Why does the admittedly inarticulate President George W. Bush enjoy communications victories that often overwhelm his adversaries? Meanwhile, war hero John F. Kerry finds his patriotism under attack in the 2004 election at the same time that Bush, who was thousands of miles from Vietnam during that war, is popularly linked to American military bravado.

And what are the differences between damage control for a big company and that for a high-profile individual? A hysterical celebrity who awakens his crisis manager at midnight often just wants to be told that he will still be adored regardless of his actual behavior. But a company needs to make money. Money can always be made discreetly, out of the limelight, while mass adoration inherently requires media coverage. The rules of damage control apply to Sunset Boulevard differently than they do to Wall Street.

Damage Control answers these and other questions from the perspective of world-weary crisis managers, not wishful-thinking academics. This is a no-holds-barred practical guide geared toward those who want to learn about the harsh realities of crisis management, not those who necessarily want to "make it" in the conventional public relations industry.

The mission of this book is to dispense with the dogma and impart the basic "facts of life" about modern crisis management—what works, what doesn't, and why. These are basic lessons passed on by authors who have spent their careers managing the nastiest public relations battles imaginable.

This book reflects the way things really are, not how we wish them to be. Life-and-death public relations struggles are not about information, as the industry repeatedly preaches. They are about power.

We endorse a political model of crisis management versus the more conventional public relations approach. The fundamental difference is that the political model, which is practiced in our hometown of Washington, D.C., assumes the threat of motivated adversaries, while the public relations model tends to view crises as organic and resolvable through good communications. In real crises there are often opponents—a mirror image of your own crisis management team—that want to torpedo you. That opposing team consists of competitors, plaintiffs' lawyers, the news media, politicians and regulators, short-sellers, multi-million-dollar nongovernmental organizations (NGOs), corporate stalkers, whistleblowers, and bloggers. These opponents don't care whether you "do the right thing"; they care about defeating you.

CHAPTER 1

The Tylenol Case Isn't the Model for Every Crisis

What began as J&J's darkest hour turned out to be its brightest in terms of corporate reputation.

—LARRY FOSTER, CORPORATE VICE-PRESIDENT OF PUBLIC RELATIONS DURING THE TYLENOL TRAGEDIES

We sometimes play a parlor game before meeting a prospective client: We take bets on how long it will take until someone associated with the client invokes the autumn 1982 Tylenol cyanide-tampering case as the model they'd like to see emulated in a proposed damage-control initiative. Bonus points are awarded in the event that someone at the table actually claims to have worked on the crisis, in which seven people—including three in one family—were killed when they took Tylenol laced with cyanide.

It's not that Johnson & Johnson, Tylenol's manufacturer, didn't effectively handle the fallout from the homicides. It's that the case study has been hyperapplied like a medieval elixir to situations that have little or nothing in common with the legendary crisis.

Just over a week after the cyanide deaths were first reported at the end of September 1982, J&J recalled and destroyed 31 million capsules at a cost of $100 million. The company's chairman, James Burke, appeared in television ads and at news conferences informing consumers of the company's actions. Tamper-resistant packaging was rapidly introduced within weeks of the murders, accompanied by a huge advertising campaign to demonstrate the new technology.

Everybody likes the Tylenol case because it involved a famous product and had a happy ending for the company. Academics use the model because it's teachable and validates the ethic of social responsibility: that "acting responsibly" is always rewarded by the marketplace. Public relations people love the Tylenol case study because it suggests there is a proprietary technique—one that they happen to know—for resolving crises. This technique inevitably includes the merits of expressing concern for consumers (which should be obvious) and, more important, the supposed benefit of the "instant" product recall.

In the months following the crisis period, J&J officials gave speeches and interviews about the case, seeking—and receiving—communications industry awards. Shortly after the murders, chief executive Burke was interviewed by CBS's *60 Minutes* in an uncharacteristically laudatory segment for the confrontational news program. Tylenol sales swiftly bounced back to near pre-crisis levels even though the killer was never found. Given the damage the murders could have done to the brand, this result was—and remains—extraordinary.

There is much to learn from Johnson & Johnson's crisis management, but blindly worshipping at this altar may be little more than an exercise in self-delusion for companies that find themselves in the crosshairs of an anxious public, a hostile media, and regulators under extraordinary pressure to make an example of bad industrial actors.

A QUESTION OF PROVENANCE

The tampering almost surely was the work of a psychopathic killer external to J&J. That the origin of the wicked act was not J&J was the key variable setting the foundation for its recovery. A company attacked by a criminal will be forgiven far more quickly than one accused of *being* the criminal. J&J's actions were admirable but logical. People were killed, so the company pulled the product from stores and encouraged consumers to throw it away.

The Tylenol case falls into a category we call a *sniper-fire crisis*—one that is caused by an outside force, like a deranged killer. Nobody's rooting for the sniper. Consumers intuitively understand that the executives of J&J didn't convene in an underground bunker to hatch a plan to harm consumers. The public might be willing to believe that a company is capable of negligence or penny-pinching irresponsibility, but in J&J's case the crimes were simply too horrific for rational people to believe that a corporation that had staked its reputation on consumer goodwill for almost a century would want something like this to happen.

As with any compelling story, the public demands instant archetypes, especially villains and victims. People process their intuition using a very specific template, one that factors in the cornerstone of Western legal and social ethics: intent. In the Tylenol case, J&J was, in addition to those who lost their lives, immediately—and instinctively—perceived as a victim, not the perpetrator of the crime.

The corporate scandals that dominate today's news are mostly of a different strain: The company's very *character* is on trial—for making faulty products or betraying the public trust. The company *is* the villain in this scenario. While it was inconceivable that J&J would knowingly harm its consumers, the recent spate of product liability and financial malfeasance scandals are all intuitively plausible.

Ford and Firestone were accused of knowingly manufacturing dangerous trucks and tires. Merck and Pfizer had to answer hard questions about the potentially deadly side effects as well as the efficacy of their arthritis drugs Vioxx and Celebrex, respectively. WorldCom, Tyco, Arthur Andersen, Enron, HealthSouth, and Adelphia instantly became cultural emblems of corruption as prosecutors accused company leaders of scheming to enrich themselves at the expense of others.

Character-driven crises like these—the opposite of a sniper-fire crisis—do not lend themselves to textbook solutions because they affect the economy, culture, and political landscape rather than just a discrete, if unfortunate, segment of the population. Evaporated pension funds make Americans' wrath toward scandal figures so virulent that public relations rescues are not options. The public doesn't just want answers; it wants vengeance. The facts of character-driven cases are not as relevant as what the cases come to symbolize in the public psyche.

Accounting giant Arthur Andersen took admirable steps to prevent extinction, such as forming a blue-ribbon panel with even bluer-chip names to examine what went wrong, but principals still were convicted (later overturned) of obstructing justice, and the firm went bankrupt. In 1989, Perrier, at the time the leading importer of bottled water in the U.S. market, adopted the Tylenol-inspired model of the instant recall when the chemical benzene was found in its product. It was commonly believed that benzene was a by-product of the manufacturing process or occurred naturally at the source from which Perrier water was derived. Regardless, the brand never fully recovered, and is not even among the top bottled waters in the United States today.

CRISIS MYTHOLOGY

The Tylenol affair ushered in a new wrinkle in crisis management: *Proselytizing how well the company has handled the crisis itself.* In a quasicomical twist, PR consultants with peripheral (if any) attachment to the case began sharing "their" insights in business forums, repeating the central myth of the "instant" recall. J&J's brilliant crisis management became unchallenged dogma.

Touting one's legitimate success is no sin, and, in fact, is a valuable service when public welfare is concerned, but not everybody bought the spin on the spin. Perhaps the most prominent skeptic was Jack O'Dwyer, whose newsletter has been chronicling the public relations industry for nearly forty years. Despite repeated assertions in business school textbooks and PR seminars that J&J "instantly" recalled Tylenol capsules, it actually took eight days "after the first deaths were announced and after another Tylenol poisoning was discovered in California," O'Dwyer wrote in his January 2000 newsletter.

In reality, it was retailers like CVS and Walgreen's that ceased stocking Tylenol capsules one day after the first death was reported on September 30, 1982. J&J's recall was announced on October 7, a time gap which, in the current age of 24-hour news coverage, would have been disastrous.

According to O'Dwyer, when questioned about the possible presence of cyanide in its facilities, J&J initially denied there was any stored in its manufacturing system. A day later, the company did admit that cyanide was stored in one facility for testing purposes. During the course of the investigation, this cyanide was ruled out as a possible source for internal contamination.

SAVING GRACE

A key factor that contributed to Tylenol's recovery was the introduction, within weeks of the murders, of tamper-evident packaging, which just happened to be in the J&J pipeline. This action—something the public could see and feel—convinced anxious consumers, regulators, and the media that J&J was doing something big to address the safety issue. The packaging itself was merchandized to the public through a huge advertising campaign, which defused anxiety about the tampering.

In 1986, however, a woman was killed in New York by a cyanide-laced Tylenol capsule, and more tampered capsules were pulled from the shelves in nearby stores. This incident begged a fundamental question: Was Tylenol's problem with the packaging or with the construction of the product itself? Capsules can be pulled apart, used as receptacles for foreign material, and then discreetly resealed.

Shortly after the 1986 New York murder, former J&J chairman Burke conceded that he regretted his decision not to abandon the capsule in 1982 when he'd had the chance. This admission (which probably didn't please J&J's attorneys) gives another glimpse into the thinking of the kind of leadership that solves problems. Burke didn't spin or word his reflection in legalese; he simply answered, "Yes, indeed I am," when asked if he was sorry for reintroducing the capsule format.

J&J is deservedly praised for having the triple-sealed packaging in its pipeline in 1982, but it was not a panacea. Nor is it reasonable to expect that every company under attack will have a handy new technology in its hip pocket.

OTHER VARIABLES IN J&J'S FAVOR

The first harsh lesson of crisis management is that not all clients are created equal. Some, like Johnson & Johnson, have intrinsic advantages. J&J had a long history of manufacturing popular products, especially those associated with children—"soft" items like No More Tears baby shampoo and baby powder. To be sure, J&J has done much to reinforce this image, but some companies are inherently at a disadvantage by virtue of the products they make. An oil, chemical, firearms, alcohol, or tobacco company in a crisis cannot expect to tap public affection. The objective for "villain" industries under attack is to cauterize the attack, not to persuade people to make associations that contradict what they fundamentally believe.

This is the central problem with crisis management that has been annexed by many public relations hucksters: the delusional and self-serving belief that you can spin a public that does not want to be spun. One can only persuade audiences within the confines of their psychological circuitry. People are more inclined to give a cuddly company like J&J a break than they would, say, the manufacturer of an allegedly carcinogenic pesticide.

Then there's the issue of consumer control. One of the first things we suggest to a client in a consumer crisis is that they give the consumer something to do, to put the consumer in charge. In Tylenol's case, the "control action" was simple and inexpensive (despite the specter of being killed by cyanide): Don't take the Tylenol in your medicine chest until the crisis is resolved, and throw your bottle away.

But imagine telling a woman with silicone breast implants— a product made by a chemical company, no less—to just throw 'em out. Not so easy. If you're worried about mobile phones causing cancer, just don't use them anymore. Oh, really? Try telling someone who has just bought an expensive sport utility vehicle to get rid of it when its rollover vulnerabilities are exposed. A huge, inconvenient, and costly move. And what exactly could Enron instantly recall upon its collapse? Nothing.

PLAYING THE ODDS RESPONSIBLY

Consumer product companies are faced with rumors of tampering every day. Sabotage gossip is especially rampant in the Internet Age and since 9/11. The vast majority of these reports turn out to be groundless. If every company recalled its products based on adverse event rumors, there would be no economy for consumer goods. Many times we advise clients to contain recalls discreetly and on a regional basis depending upon the credibility of the report (Internet rumors are notoriously inaccurate) and the severity of the allegation (How seriously could someone be injured?).

Responsible, educated intelligence work and odds-making address most, but not all, crisis scenarios. A company must be prepared to initiate a nation- or worldwide recall immediately, but it is logistically absurd to embrace the "instant" recall canard as the only option for besieged manufacturers.

After initial missteps, Firestone recalled its tires in 2000 and began to rebuild its brand under a new name, Bridgestone. Similarly, after a 1996 plane crash that killed 110 in Florida, ValuJet eventually regained trust by resolving what caused the crash, merging with another airline, and rebuilding under its new name, AirTran. Even ImClone, hit by the Martha Stewart torpedo, has begun to emerge from stormy seas—despite its imprisoned founder—by proving that its once-scorned cancer drug is effective after all.

One outcome that is rarely included in Tylenol lionizations is the protracted litigation between the victims' families and J&J. Eight years after the murders, J&J settled with the families for an undisclosed sum, according to O'Dwyer, "just as jury selection was to start in Cook County." That this escaped public scrutiny is a testament to J&J's damage control, management recognizing when it was time to take a deep breath and cut a check.

We've known executives who, at many companies that didn't enjoy the outcome that J&J did, beat themselves up, wondering what they did wrong. While self-criticism is healthy, the Tylenol dogma has done a disservice to enterprises trying to grapple with crisis management.

The Tylenol crisis taught us good things that responsible companies can do when confronted by murderers. While a quarter century of hindsight may suggest that J&J should have recalled the Tylenol capsules immediately and ceased their production, Monday morning quarterbacks must remember that crisis management by its very nature is about making good decisions, not perfect ones. J&J did most of the right things in a messy world littered with incomplete information.

Perhaps the true genius of the Tylenol crisis lies both in its merchandizing as well as in its actual handling. As media and business pundits proliferate, the two may prove to be equally important.

CHAPTER 2

Know the Difference Between a Nuisance, a Problem, a Crisis, and a Marketplace Assault

[Sudden acceleration] is a mysterious phenomenon in which a short, silly, middle-aged woman with a lawyer gets into an Audi 5000 and—all of a sudden, for no apparent reason—goes through the back wall of her garage and onto the CBS *60 Minutes* television program.

—P. J. O'ROURKE

In order to cure an ailment, you must first know what the ailment is. In crisis management, one of the greatest challenges lies in diagnosis. Perhaps the most common misdiagnosis in high-stakes public relations is confusing a communications problem with a conflict.

In a communications problem, some information is lacking. Education and awareness-building can cure the problem. If, for example, people are aware they are at risk for heart disease, they will be able to take tangible steps to prevent it—exercise, eat right, have regular checkups. There's no side in the conversation making an argument against better health.

But in a conflict, there are sides, with opposing agendas. In-formation isn't missing from the conversation; in fact, there's no introducible bit of information that could change the mind of one side or the other.

In these zero-sum, my-side-versus-your-side conflicts, it is a big mistake to envision the battleground as a graph in which data points are charted and the side with more impressive data wins. A real PR war is multidimensional, with conflicting facts colliding with opposing agendas and unpredictable vicissitudes.

While we call our business "crisis management," more often than not we are really navigating such *marketplace assaults,* which are different from pure crises. A crisis is a house that caught on fire because lightning struck. The event was organic, an act of nature. In a marketplace assault, someone *wanted* the house to be on fire, so they torched it (and placed incendiary devices around the house to sabotage the work of firefighters).

When a business is under a marketplace assault, often, the other side's agenda has a legitimate component. In a market-place assault, a crisis, such as a corporate bankruptcy due to scandal, meets an agenda, such as a plaintiff's attorney looking to profit from the crisis in addition to recovering his client's as-sets. In another example, the pharmaceutical industry must re-spond not only to legitimate concerns about drug safety but also to the public's outrage over corporate profits and the cost of drugs.

A case in point: A few years ago, an ostensibly "concerned citizen" began alleging online that mainstream feminine care products were harming women with residue supposedly left over from the manufacturing process. It was an allegation that had to be taken seriously because in 1980, women died from toxic shock syndrome, a disease associated with a tampon product that is no longer on the market. Some within the brand manufacturing companies wanted to address these new allegations as a crisis, believing that a public education campaign explaining the falsity of this person's claims would prove the allegations were unfounded.

The problem with this approach was that the "activist" spreading the rumors was not an ordinary citizen. She was, in fact, affiliated with the manufacturer of an "organic" tampon product competing for market share, and she was launching a marketplace assault. This motivated adversary was financially vested in the argument that branded products (e.g., Tampax, Kotex, Playtex) were hazardous, and no amount of "public education" was going to change that.

Once we realized what our client was up against, we suggested abandoning the crisis management strategy of product-attribute public education. Some within our client's company bristled, having already convinced themselves that such a campaign would improve their company's PR. As crisis managers, however, we are loyal to our client's well-being, not to a strategy. We believe in being flexible and are willing to abandon strategies when the operating climate changes. Eventually, with some convincing, we shifted our focus to exposing the smear apparatus that had been cynically created to scare women into buying the organic product. The consumer media, to its credit, became outraged to learn they had been misled by the organic company's guerrilla campaign. The bad news about brand-name tampons eventually went away and sales of brand feminine-care products recovered. Much of the effort's ultimate success was due to our client's trust and willingness to cast aside a strategy that was management's favorite earlier in the process.

For the most part, a marketplace assault must be navigated, not "managed"—an arrogant notion that falsely assumes that you, as the principal, are in total control of your destiny. You're not; you're only in control of your role in a series of collisions between dynamic variables—quantifiable hazards, agendas, personalities, politics, the mood of the culture.

IN PRAISE OF BLAME?

Blame exists for a reason: It's useful.

"The human impulse to blame grows out of the evolutionary need to avert harm," observed Ohio University professor Mark Alicke. In other words, we are hardwired to single out those who may pose a danger to the rest of us, whether deserved or not. Blame employs shame as a punishment to those who are perceived to have failed to serve the community at large; it is a cultural survival mechanism.

Our rational selves understand, for example, that one man should not be blamed for a hurricane, but that's very much what happened to Federal Emergency Management Agency chief Michael Brown in the aftermath of Hurricane Katrina. As Brown became the personification of bureaucratic negligence, President Bush apologized to the nation for the government's poor response, then accelerated aid to the devastated region—one good thing that sprung from blame in this instance.

There's something "in" blame for everybody. Blame is

essentially a service to the community. Blame punishes the few in the best interests of the many. It allows a selected scapegoat to bear the brunt of punishment so that the rest of us can smugly proceed with our lives.

When the opportunity to blame isn't present, a potentially difficult situation may stay at the nuisance or problem level. When the potential for blame is high, the situation is more likely to erupt into a crisis or marketplace assault.

It's therefore a waste of precious resources to attempt to enlighten an enraged population about cause-and-effect or other fine points when they are in an emotional uproar. Human beings understand the world in terms of archetypal narratives—stories with clear villains and victims and vindicators—and effective crisis management must accept that.

A CAUTIONARY TALE:
HOW AUDI GOT SIDESWIPED

On November 23, 1986, the media introduced Americans to a compelling cast of characters and a blockbuster narrative. This murder mystery featured a reverend and his wife, their six-year-old boy, and his murderer: a seemingly possessed automobile, the Audi 5000.

This narrative came via CBS's *60 Minutes,* the television news magazine program known for its hard-hitting investigative reports. In the aptly titled segment "Out of Control," an understandably distraught Kristi Bradosky alleged that her Audi 5000 lurched forward in her garage, unprompted, killing her young son, Joshua:

Bradosky: I got back into the car and put my foot on the brake to put it in drive, and the car surged forward, and I saw that I was going to hit him. So, I put my foot on the brake [again], but it didn't stop the car. (Crying) It pushed him through the garage. And we had a panel partition, and it went through the partition. He went through it. (Crying)

Ed Bradley (CBS): You put your foot on the brake.

Bradosky: Mm-hmm.

Field demonstrations shown on the broadcast depicted an Audi—with no one in the driver's seat—zooming ahead. An executive of Audi of America explained the physical impossibility of the runaway car, but he was overwhelmed by a prosecutorial Ed Bradley and the audience's visceral identification with Bradosky's grief.

The broadcast was a disaster for Audi, and a new mechanical syndrome, "sudden acceleration," was born. No matter how hard a driver pressed down on the brake, the car would keep zooming ahead, Audi owners insisted.

We played a small and invisible role in this drama. We were young executives working for a communications consulting firm that had been assigned to the Audi case. One of our assignments was to track all of the local news reports of "me-too" incidents of runaway Audis that proliferated across the country in the days following the *60 Minutes* broadcast. Local media outlets began picking up on the same narrative—*the car just took off by itself!*—and broadcasting their own versions of the Bradosky saga, though none had resulted in a death.

We vividly remember explaining to an investigative reporter in a Boston newsroom (who had located her own set of victims) that the car's brake can always override the accelerator. In a statement that has haunted us for twenty years, the reporter pointed to the camera, and said, "But *they* don't know that." What did she mean? That it was her job to educate the public? Or the opposite . . . that it was her job to validate a preexisting belief independent of the facts?

Despite these questions, we remembered the admonition of our superiors: Be nice. After all, we were dealing with a story driven by a woman whose grief was legitimate even if her version of events was questionable.

The *60 Minutes* report was a blockbuster news story. Government investigations began. A support group, closely linked with plaintiffs' attorneys, sprouted up. Called the Audi Victims Network, they soon were selling T-shirts. Audi, for its part, was assertive in defending its product but was committed to its public relations mantra: Be nice. Be nice.

CBS repeated the broadcast in September of the following year with an update citing 1,200 reports of sudden acceleration, including 5 deaths and 400 injuries. The supposedly mechanical syndrome became sufficiently accepted as real, and it began mysteriously migrating to other automobiles involved in crashes.

By the end of 1987, the Audi matter was more in need of attorneys than it was public relations people.

We remember being stunned a few years later to learn that *all* the people who sued Audi lost their cases, including the Bradoskys. Kristi Bradosky, whose tragic story was the emotional locomotive of the marketplace assault, later admitted under oath that she might have told the police officer who arrived at the scene of her accident that her foot had been on the accelerator when the accident happened, a very different scenario from sudden acceleration. Another woman, who was featured in the *60 Minutes* report "teaser," was later fined $20,000 for filing a frivolous lawsuit.

In 1989, when the Audi furor had subsided, the government's National Highway Traffic Safety Administration, spurred into action by *60 Minutes*'s Audi segment, released a report concluding that there was no mechanical basis for "sudden acceleration," and said most of the accidents were probably caused by driver error. The drivers had most likely placed their foot on the accelerator.

It also came to light that the *60 Minutes* footage of the suddenly accelerating Audi had been choreographed by an automotive consultant who remotely fed fluid into the transmission, thus rigging the car's televised lurch. Litigation expert Walter Olson wrote in the *National Review,* "The tank with its attached hose was apparently sitting right on the front passenger seat of the doctored Audi, but the *60 Minutes* cameras managed not to pick it up."

Despite the failure of one single allegation of sudden acceleration to hold up in court, Audi's sales didn't recover for more than a decade. The company had lost "billions," according to one executive. Audi sales, which had peaked at 74,000 the year before the *60 Minutes* broadcast, plunged to an annual average of 14,000 in the early 1990s, a market share loss of more than 80 percent.

"We had a choice of suing [*60 Minutes*]," said Philip Hutchinson, an Audi official, years after the episode. "If we had won, it would have been a Pyrrhic victory. If we had won, what would Audi's sales have been?"

THE LESSONS

Human nature makes us want to find fault in hindsight with how things were handled, and, surely, error can always be found. In the case of the alleged sudden acceleration of Audis, however, what became clear early on was that converging forces were creating an environment ripe for blame: sympathetic victims; a compelling narrative; a scary and not-readily-explained phenomenon; public outrage and hysteria; a spontaneous media feeding frenzy; consumers with the time, energy, and money to litigate; opportunistic plaintiffs' lawyers.

Audi, a German company whose motto at the time was "The Art of Engineering," attempted to fight back on the only wavelength it understood: the Facts. The audience, however, wasn't processing information; it was processing emotions. Anxious people, by nature, don't ask, "What are the facts?" They ask, "Whom do I identify with?" In a battle between a grieving mother and the laws of physics, tears overpower statistics.

Barely a week has gone by in the twenty-plus years since the Audi debacle that we don't wonder what might have been done differently. We are not convinced that all of the resources (plus all the hindsight) in the world could have pulled Audi out of the *60 Minutes* debacle. Sometimes the forces lined up against a company are simply too strong, even against a deft strategy deployed by clever handlers. Failure is failure, regardless of its cause. Lessons, however, can still be learned.

In retrospect, the greatest lesson of the Audi affair is that when an avalanche of blame is inevitable, unconventional methods of response must be entertained. Does it pay, for example, for a company to embrace the public relations industry's consistent advice to convey warmth and caring in the face of an attack by bitterly motivated adversaries? Part of the reason for adopting a conciliatory position is the hope that your critics will treat you more humanely. But what if your critics come to view your niceness as a sign of weakness and attack even harder? In the Audi case, there was no correlation between how much empathy the company conveyed to its critics and a cessation in hostilities. In today's adversarial climate, if you believe you are being wrongly attacked, hitting hard and hitting first should be high on your list of options.

There is also a lesson to be learned in paying attention to changes in the cultural and technological climate. In 1986, *60 Minutes* was the gold standard of television journalism. There was nowhere else to go, no media court of appeals. The other network programs ran with the same kind of narrative: Villain (Audi); Victim (Joshua Bradosky); and Vindicator (Ed Bradley).

Today there's another media game in town—games, actually. There are numerous networks, blogs, and other media that one can approach in a marketplace assault. We now know not to trust theater arranged by television networks that have their own competitive agenda. While *60 Minutes* never had to apologize for its rigged Audi test despite the damage it caused, *Dateline NBC* and its top executives were badly embarrassed in 1992 when the show's producers chose to demonstrate the flammability of a vehicle by rigging it with explosives.

Today communicators can introduce alternative narratives, including indelicate ones that require self-styled victims to pay a serious price if their stories fail to hold water. In the case of sud-

den acceleration, this would have included a m
paign to discredit the alleged "victims."

Litigation against a media outlet, which wo
deemed unthinkable in 1986 on the grounds that "it's too
messy," is now fair game when an entire company is on the line.
Moreover, with recent media debacles and the retirement of
old-line standard-bearers such as CBS News's Dan Rather, news
organizations are more self-critical than they were in the 1980s,
which is a net positive for aggrieved parties.

For every activist group that emerges to attack a product, a
new—and equally legitimate—grassroots group can be mobilized to challenge it. Grievance groups, while often anchored in
respectable desires, are sometimes corrupted by the agendas of
trial attorneys and the whims of media cycles. One of the prime
movers in the attack on Audi was the Ralph Nader–founded
Center for Auto Safety. Nader's reputation for doing good works
aside, the organization was shameless in its trafficking in the canard of sudden acceleration.

There was a time when any attack on a business target was
considered noble and any defense somehow underhanded because of the taint of profit making. The attackers no longer wear
the impenetrable mantle of virtue that they once did, and the
consumer media, beholden to an antibusiness ideology from the
1960s through the 1990s, now, because of a series of journalistic
debacles, recognize that not all journalism that results in the destruction of an enterprise is good journalism.

Perhaps the antiquated, gentler school of public relations
plays an important role in confronting nuisances and problems.
But when a crisis or marketplace assault comes courting, the old

elixirs should be relegated to the memories of a simpler time when the stakes were lower. Where there was once deference in the face of a crisis and marketplace assault, there now is resistance. And there should be.

HEWLETT-PACKARD: OVERKILL IN CRISIS MANAGEMENT

If ever there were a case of failing to differentiate between a nuisance, a problem, and a crisis, it was the bungled 2006 attempt by Hewlett-Packard's top brass to ferret out boardroom leaks by spying on their own board of directors, among others. In this notorious sin of excess, the cure became worse than the disease.

The scandal's climax came in the form of congressional hearings in which ten witnesses invoked their Fifth Amendment right against self-incrimination—sinister optics that helped turn a problem (a leaky board) into a crisis (Nixonian dirty tricks).

By most accounts, in late 2005 HP chairman Patricia Dunn set in motion a private investigation that resulted in, among other things, the collection of the private phone records of nine journalists, two HP employees, and seven HP board members. These records were gathered via the use of "pretexting." Pretexting is gathering information through misrepresentation—in the case of the HP scandal, pretending to be the person to whom those private phone records belonged. As Representative Joe Barton (R-TX) said at the congressional hearing, "Pretexting is pretending to be somebody you're not to get something you probably shouldn't have to use in a way that's probably wrong." These revelations came to light in early September 2006.

Dunn, who was indicted for fraud and conspiracy the following month, was not fundamentally wrong to be concerned about boardroom leaks. As CEO Mark Hurd said upon her resignation: "The intent of the investigation was proper and appropriate. The fact that we had leaks on the board needed to be resolved." The problem was that her team appeared to have been obsessed to the point of monomania.

Nor was Dunn wrong to entertain the use of private investigators, a practice that is indiscriminately branded as unethical in today's scandal climate. Some private investigations, dare we say, are good things. Without investigators, General Motors never would have learned that journalists at *Dateline NBC* had rigged a GM truck to explode in order to portray an alleged pattern of flammability. Indeed, our own experience has been that private investigations can identify and stop bad actors who have no God-given right to ignore the law in pursuit of their corporate quarry.

The problem with HP's actions was that they were undertaken without seasoned leadership, and whatever flimsy parameters were set apparently cascaded out of control and came to include tactics and targets that should have been off-limits. In an unheeded e-mail, HP internal investigator Vince Nye wrote to his supervisor, "I am requesting that we cease this phone number gathering method immediately and discount any of its information."

There is such a thing as overresponding to a threat, which is what HP did when confronted by leaks. While as of this writing the facts of the case are still unfolding, one thing is certain: The operation that was put in place to plug the leaks did more damage to HP than the leaks ever did.

Excess also can reign when companies try to correct a misstep. The resignations of HP's general counsel, chief ethics officer, and a security manager weren't considered sufficient by some in the news media. Pundits were calling for a complete housecleaning at HP, unwisely believing that overkill was the answer. In reality, sometimes the best people to lead a company through a crisis are the ones who have already demonstrated strong leadership. Leaving a company in crisis without a leader would likely spin it even deeper into crisis. It should not be the objective of a company under siege to satisfy the bloodlust of the news media or business pundits, who are notorious for equating drastic gestures of self-flagellation with good crisis management.

"Tell it all," "Get it all out," went the extreme chants of the scandal's Greek chorus in the weeks before HP spoke publicly. One problem with these absolutes is that companies in crisis rarely know everything they need to know in order to make immediate and ideal decisions. That's why it's a crisis.

Another problem is that complete disclosures, while theoretically desirable, may be admissible in court and can place the company in legal jeopardy. If HP had begun speculating publicly about who did what, innocent people could have been smeared, forcing them to take legal action against the company. Moreover, HP didn't want to give fodder to prosecutors who were investigating the matter. Herein lies the tension between attorneys, who tend to counsel silence, and communicators, who tend to counsel openness. Who's right? Both are "right" within the context of their disciplines; however, each crisis has its own special set of considerations. It's up to the chief crisis officer (usually the CEO) to determine where on the silence-openness continuum public statements must fall.

On Friday, September 22, 2006, HP CEO Mark Hurd held a news conference (but took no questions) in which, for the first time since the affair broke in the press several weeks earlier, he commented at some length on the scandal and announced the resignation of chairman Dunn. Hurd also apologized to those who were spied upon and announced the appointment of former U.S. prosecutor Bart Schwartz to look into the investigative methods that were employed by the company in its attempt to plug leaks. (Presumably, this action will result in a final report on who did what—and pave the way for a clearer policy on corporate investigations.)

Also at the news conference, Michael Holston of Morgan, Lewis & Bockius, a law firm HP retained to investigate what actually transpired, reported on the pathology of the scandal, namely that telephone records of employees, directors, and journalists had been obtained via the use of pretexting.

Was Hurd's news conference held too late? In a perfect world, sure; but in the real world where a leader needs to know what he's talking about, it was the best of his bad options.

Hurd was criticized for not taking questions, but he was probably wise not to. When legal issues are at stake—especially when information is so limited—open-ended give-and-take with the news media is laden with mines. In the proverbial battle between lawyers and public relations people, the HP press conference was a thoughtful compromise between the two disciplines.

At the time of the congressional hearings on the scandal in 2006, HP's shares were up 25 percent. Key corporate units, such as HP's printing products, which had been faltering, have recovered under Hurd. Analysts rightly remain bullish on the stock despite the leak scandal, which, in the end, had nothing to do with the company's fundamental businesses.

CHAPTER 3

Blame and Resentment

Fault, *n.* One of my offenses, as different from one of yours, the latter being crimes.

—AMBROSE BIERCE,
THE DEVIL'S DICTIONARY

The media pursue two dueling narratives in organizational crises: the victims' plight, and the tale of an embattled CEO. Whether it's Coca-Cola or Hurricane Katrina, these archetypes—a vulnerable victim pitted against an arrogant or incompetent villain—are inevitably polarized to fit the prefabricated format that the mass audience can easily process. There are few emotions more powerful than the urge to blame. If there is a suffering victim, there *must* be a villain who either purposely caused it, or didn't do enough to stop it. The contrast is the key to the explosiveness of the story—after all, one cannot simultaneously have innocent victims and villains . . . who are trying their gosh-darned best.

The Scylla and Charybdis of crisis management are blame and resentment, and all crises need to be evaluated against these deadly twins.

As domestic diva Martha Stewart became embroiled in an insider trading scandal, some pundits argued that her alleged crime was minor relative to other scandals that were making their way into the public dockets.

The fact is, even with the steady drumbeat of corporate malfeasance stories, Martha Stewart's scandal is the only narrative that the public and consumer media understood. Even the amount at stake, $45,000, was easily digestible, as opposed to the $100 billion collapse of WorldCom. As the stock market stalled, corporate scandals multiplied, and ludicrous wealth hemorrhaged into the hands of Silicon Valley upstarts, Martha Stewart was a convenient icon upon whom blame and resentment could be easily projected.

Coca-Cola was widely blamed for mishandling a crisis that germanated from deeper cultural resentments. On June 8, 1999, the head of the St. Mary School in Brussels sent thirty-three of his middle school students to the hospital when they complained of dizziness, nausea, and vomiting. This headmaster, Odilon Hermans, suspected food poisoning. Hermans began to focus on Coca-Cola when he became aware that students were consuming the soft drink in higher numbers thanks to a contest involving a promotional message under the bottle cap. Hermans contacted the plant in Antwerp and requested that the remaining Coke cases be removed from his school. The company sent several representatives but did not remove the bottles. Finally, on day three of the crisis, the company finally removed the remaining cases, although it attributed the illnesses to coincidence. "We had to push them a little bit," Hermans said.

As Cokes were being taken away from the St. Mary School on June 10, schoolchildren in another Belgian city were falling ill supposedly from canned Coca-Cola and fruit-flavored Fanta. These Coke products were manufactured at a different plant from the one that supplied the St. Mary School. Similar reports began to surface in France, the Netherlands, and Luxemburg. About fifty additional schoolchildren were hospitalized in these countries. Incredibly, a U.S.-based spokesperson said, "It may make you feel sick, but it is not harmful." Coca-Cola's chief executive, Douglas Ivester, who was traveling in Europe, was told that the outbreaks were not serious, and he returned to Atlanta as panic swept Europe.

Coca-Cola products were being pulled from stores and vending machines, and the lenses of the worldwide news media were on hand to film the rise of overseas outrage. The narrative essentially juxtaposed sick children with a wealthy American CEO hightailing it out of Europe on a private jet. Ivester remained at corporate headquarters in Atlanta throughout the crisis, and many of the key communications emanated from Atlanta.

Belgian national elections were held three days after the second round of illnesses were reported, and the country tossed its leaders from office, replacing them with a new government. The new Belgian minister of health was notoriously anti-American (and the European public was already alarmed by the prospect of having their beloved food supply "tainted" by U.S.-grown genetically modified foods). The minister established a hotline for consumers to report adverse incidents involving Coke products.

Coca-Cola initiated a massive, multination recall as investigations of contaminated products got under way. Coke products were banned in Belgium, Luxembourg, and the Netherlands.

Coca-Cola attributed the illnesses to causes ranging from contaminated carbon dioxide to psychosomatic hysteria. On a clinical level, they may have been right. On an emotional frequency—the wavelength that matters in times of crisis—they were wrong. The sicknesses occurred during a witch hunt climate against the food industry in Europe. Headlines had already been replete with references to mad cow disease and other concerns.

Coke CEO Ivester issued a vague apology to Belgians in a print advertising campaign. Apologies are often positioned as a panacea in crisis management; however, once they actually happen, people are rarely impressed. "Too little, too late" is often the reaction, as it was in Belgium when Coca-Cola's self-serving apology was released from Atlanta, in part reading:

> We deeply regret any problems experienced by our European consumers. The Coca-Cola Company's highest priority is the quality of our products. For 113 years our success has been based on the trust that consumers have in that quality. That trust is sacred to us.

"Yeah, but," Europeans said, "if that trust were so sacred, what were you doing bolting from the Continent on your Gulfstream when the crisis went down?"

Belgium allowed Coca-Cola products back into the country about one week later, after no tangible evidence of tainted products was found, but business analysts fell all over themselves to pillory Coke for the company's mismanagement. Just five months after the scare, Ivester was fired. The European situation was widely perceived as a contributing factor in the management shake-up.

Conventional wisdom would attribute Coca-Cola's mistake to its slowness to recall its products, given that the post-Tylenol cliché is that one must immediately recall a product if there's a perceived problem with it. This always-recall aphorism may seem like a tidy policy in a PowerPoint presentation, but the reality is that if it were followed, big companies would be doing nothing but recalling their products.

Where Ivester and Coca-Cola went wrong was turning a deaf ear to the political sentiment in Europe, one of brewing anti-Americanism and suspicion of the food industry. The company, which is politically savvy in most regions of the world, failed to appreciate the degree to which resentment can trigger a witch hunt. The mightiest institutions ironically become the most vulnerable under such conditions. When outrage takes over, there is no emotion more powerful than the urge to place blame, and Coke found itself the beneficiary of an entire continent's wrath for a nonlethal problem.

Under calmer social conditions, the company might, on a purely odds-making level, have been correct not to regard the initial reports as a potential crisis. However, given the preexisting level of anxiety about food issues and the anti-American sentiment, the company's response was inadequate. Coke didn't realize that Europeans had reason to vilify them.

———

Everybody should love the pharmaceutical industry. After all, it's in the business of curing us and helping us live longer and better.

But the industry has been on the receiving end of a consumer and government insurrection. While the new millennium has awarded drug companies record profits, the cost to their reputations has been severe. According to some surveys, they are more hated than the tobacco and oil industries, an ironic position since many of the same people who loathe Big Pharma don't dispute that the industry does a lot of good.

Since in one corner there are sick people suffering, while a corporation is making profits while curing them in another, there's an easy victim and a villain: The pharmaceutical industry is seen as a rapacious, immoral juggernaut that ends up hurting its fellow man.

More than anything else, consumers don't want to pay high prices for drugs. Outrage is especially intense among people on fixed incomes who argue that in some cases, they are being forced to choose between medicine and food. The drug companies' record profits are bitterly resented against this backdrop. Some people are offended that drug companies have enough money to advertise. Shouldn't all of the money being spent on direct-to-consumer advertisements be used for research and development?

After being saturated with promises of the perfect lives medicines can render, consumers are disappointed that their wildest curative dreams sometimes fail to materialize, and that they're still suffering. Hostility toward drug companies is especially intense when patients come face-to-face with risk—risk that the drug will have dangerous side effects or that it just might not work—a nonnegotiable no-no in contemporary life. Still others fume that health is an entitlement, not a luxury item to be dispensed on an à la carte basis.

In early 2004, this entitlement clashed with reality when the Food and Drug Administration found evidence that the psychoactive drugs Paxil (from GlaxoSmithKline) and Effexor (from Wyeth) may raise the risk of suicide in young patients. In June, New York state attorney general Eliot Spitzer sued GSK claiming that the drug maker withheld negative clinical trial data about its increased suicide risk. In August, GSK reached a settlement with Spitzer, which was followed shortly thereafter by congressional hearings about the potential hazards of antidepressants in children. If *these* drugs hadn't been adequately tested, many reasoned, what else were they hiding from us?

In September 2004, the resentments against drug companies were validated when pharmaceutical giant Merck pulled its blockbuster arthritis drug Vioxx from the marketplace, citing risks to patients of heart attack and stroke. The drug, which was used by millions, was prescribed so widely because it was both effective and spared patients the gastrointestinal discomfort associated with arthritis drugs. Merck's stock was hit hard by an unforgiving marketplace, its stock plunging 26 percent on the news.

With institutional crises, visceral outrage is always followed by the emergence of telltale what-did-they-know-and-when-did-they-know-it documents. Merck was to be no exception: Documents soon surfaced suggesting that Merck leadership rejected plans to conduct a study of heart risks as early as 1997. Business coverage immediately speculated on the job security of

CEO Raymond Gilmartin, the strong implication being that Merck would be well served by a high-level purge.

Merck's fourth-quarter 2004 earnings dropped 21 percent, and losses for that time period were estimated at $750 million. Merrill Lynch estimated that the company's losses associated with the Vioxx recall would run between $4 billion and $18 billion.

Adding insult to injury, one public opinion poll indicated that only 9 percent of the public felt that drug companies could be trusted. In the months following the Vioxx recall, a whistleblower from within the Food and Drug Administration, Dr. David Graham, associate director for science and medicine in the Office of Drug Safety, testified before a Senate committee about the broader context:

> It is important that this committee and the American people understand that what happened with Vioxx is really a symptom of something far more dangerous to the safety of the American people.

Graham named five additional products he believed deserved the scrutiny and punishment that befell Vioxx, including weight-loss drug Meridia, the statin Crestor, the acne drug Accutane, Serevent for asthma, and the painkiller Bextra. Shortly after AstraZeneca's Crestor was pilloried in the press, a scientific study showed that it was the first statin to actually show a regression in arterial plaque.

In January 2006, *Consumer Reports* ran a scathing article about drug safety subtitled "FDA: From Watchdog to Lapdog." This hemorrhage of ill will manifested itself in the form of 2,300 product liability lawsuits against Merck from 4,600 plaintiff groups. CEO Gilmartin stepped down.

The first major Vioxx trial reflected the bad publicity that surrounded it. In July 2005, a Texas jury found Merck negligent in the death of fifty-nine-year-old Robert Ernst, who had died in 2001, six months after first taking Vioxx. His widow was awarded $253 million.

Merck enjoyed a different outcome several months later when a jury absolved the company of any role in the death of a sixty-year-old Idaho man. The jury decided that Merck had properly warned the patient, who had multiple signs of cardiovascular disease, of the risks of Vioxx. In February 2006, a federal jury declared that Merck was not responsible for the fatal heart attack of a man who had taken Vioxx for less than a month.

There is a valuable lesson in these victories: The same search for balance that wrought antipharmaceutical sentiment may put a halt to abusive lawsuits if the spotlight can be shone on plaintiffs' attorneys. Juries see themselves as cultural messengers, not arbiters of small-scale, case-by-case justice. The proverbial drug company that harms innocent people may be ripe for punishment, but a patient who takes a calculated risk in search of a better life may not be uniquely deserving of vast riches.

Many corporate damage-control campaigns are doomed from the beginning because of the marketing template the architects use for planning. The main flaw of the marketing template is that it assumes that the company can control the crisis as it controls the life cycle of the product: design, manufacture, launch, distribution, and advertising. In a category five crapstorm, make no mistake about it: The crisis is controlling you.

CHAPTER 4

Offense Wins, Defense Loses

The greatest weakness of the commander who does not take the initiative, either in planning or attack, lies in his continual search for something, or indeed anything, to react to. He is therefore vulnerable to the ploys of his opponent.

—*THE CAMBRIDGE ILLUSTRATED HISTORY OF WARFARE*

State attorneys general wield frightening powers—and no one more so than New York's former AG, Eliot Spitzer. Backed by an army of 500 state attorneys, the implicit support of the tort bar, and an ever-attentive press corps, "The High Executioner of Wall Street" (as the *Wall Street Journal* dubbed him) launched legal-PR blitzkriegs that were designed to bring his targets to their knees long before any prospect of an actual court appearance. It was the classic school-yard bully ploy: Talk tough. Swing first. And pray no one swings back.

Marsh & McLennan certainly didn't. In 2004, when Mr. Spitzer accused brokers at Marsh and other insurance companies of bid-rigging and steering contracts to preferred insurers, for which they allegedly received kickbacks, the company didn't put up much of a fight. Marsh quickly surrendered and announced it would suspend contingent commissions—a longtime accepted and arguably legitimate practice. Soon thereafter, the CEO was fired (replaced by a friend of Mr. Spitzer), the stock price dropped 40 percent, and 3,000 workers were laid off. Much of the same happened at insurance giant AIG, where 11 days after a Spitzer attack the board caved in to the pressure, failed to contest any of the allegations, and tossed overboard its longtime CEO, the venerable Hank Greenberg. Even though Spitzer ultimately dropped his criminal charges against Greenberg, the media die was cast and the damage to his reputation was done.

Just months earlier, Wall Street's biggest securities firms had settled with the attorney general over his allegations that they were peddling biased stock research. His bounty: fines totaling a whopping $1.4 billion, the fruits of a yearlong pressure campaign. And so it went on Mr. Spitzer's Wall Street: Call a press conference, launch a lawsuit, vilify the CEO, drive down the stock price, force capitulation. The Spitzer Reign of Terror.

Then the tide began to turn, as it often does, because a few brave souls decided it was time to stand up to the bully, to get off the back foot and go on the offensive.

When Mr. Spitzer decided in May of 2004 to take on New York Stock Exchange chairman Richard Grasso over his $187 million pay package, suing not only Mr. Grasso but also NYSE director Kenneth Langone, Spitzer got a taste of his own medicine. Messrs. Grasso and Langone, two men with the means and the muscle to stand up to him, fired back. Said Langone: "You tell

Spitzer that if he's going to try this case, he should try it himself because my lawyers will beat him like a rented mule." Said Grasso: ". . . Spitzer's decision to intervene in a commercial dispute between the New York Stock Exchange and me over my compensation and retirement benefits smacks of politics." Said Langone: "Accustomed to bullying settlements, mistaking bluster for substance, Mr. Spitzer apparently expects I will capitulate, to the tune of $18 million. But his claims are false and his suit will fail." Said Grasso: "Those who thought they could break me with their repeated media leaks badly underestimated my character and resolve. I look forward to addressing them in court where they can no longer hide behind Mr. Spitzer's cloak." Grasso and Langone were not simply responding to the AG's attacks, they were launching a few of their own.

But over time, it wasn't just well-heeled tough guys like Grasso and Langone who were pushing back. Conservatively managed publicly traded companies such as H&R Block also went on the offensive in response to Mr. Spitzer's charges. In early 2006, at the height of tax-filing season—when media interest would be greatest—Attorney General Spitzer charged the company with fraudulently selling retirement savings plans. He threatened the company with "vast fines" unless it capitulated. It didn't. First, H&R Block let the media know that, despite the attorney general's blustery threats of a $250 million fine, he had privately offered to settle for as little as $30 million—and the company had rejected it. It also fired back tit-for-tat in the media: "That the Attorney General's office has chosen to ignore the facts, rely on information taken out of context, and continues to attack our company and our product seems tailored to objectives other than the merits of the case. . . . I [the company's CEO] use the words 'unfair attack' deliberately, for that is exactly what I believe we are facing."

With his targets turning the tables and going from defense to offense, the bully of Wall Street found the going tougher when he sought to win lawsuits through intimidation versus trying them in court on their merits.

INTRODUCING RISK TO YOUR ATTACKER

Offense nearly always trumps defense for several reasons. First, the news media are allegation-driven. Whoever is alleging is shaping the coverage. News reports lead with an allegation; to the extent "the other side" is included, it typically comes much later in the story. Getting to reporters first with your perspective doesn't guarantee you positive coverage, but it does significantly increase your chances. Let's be frank: If you are on the receiving end of an allegation and you hear from the press, in most cases their story is 90 percent written before they even call you.

Second, we are conditioned to believe innocent people don't run or hide from a problem, an accuser, or a crisis. O. J. Simpson, streaking down an L.A. freeway in his infamous white Bronco, trying to evade helicopters and squad cars for mile after mile, isn't exactly sending a reassuring signal that he's got nothing to hide. The public, the news media, politicians, and other audiences read body language as much as they do a carefully worded corporate statement. Equivocation spawns suspicion. Silence equals guilt. A passionless response to an unfounded attack makes one wonder how strongly the accused believes in his or her own innocence.

Third, playing defense requires far more resources and is vastly less efficient than playing offense. Digging trenches and hoisting sandbags takes a lot more energy than tossing grenades. By making the other side play defense, you force them to consume time and money figuring out what hit them and what to do about it. If they're locked away in meeting rooms and on conference calls bickering about how to respond to your offensive, they sure as heck aren't working on launching one of their own.

Finally, a demonstrated ability to throw punches sends an invaluable message to your adversary that their siege against you or your company "won't be easy." Most of today's professional agitators know it is wisest to go after the company with the softest backbone. They can't bring down the entire herd, so they pick on the most vulnerable. Your job is to convince them otherwise, to let them know they've picked on the wrong guy. And, surprisingly, the toughest corporate attackers often have glass jaws. They are so conditioned to attack, attack, attack that there is very little in their own personal or institutional experience that has prepared them for defense.

A HOSPITAL COUNTERPUNCHES

Take the case of a California acute-care facility facing dozens of highly questionable lawsuits. They all alleged patients had died or become extremely ill by acquiring "staph" infections while undergoing surgical procedures. The hospital felt confident the facts were on its side. It had a stellar reputation and a state-of-the-art system for controlling the spread of germs. The plaintiff's attorney had sued the hospital before, and, not surprisingly, she had inflicted far more damage through the news media than in the courts. Her implied threat this time was no different: Settle the cases or I'm going to the press. In a hotly competitive market, the charge that the hospital was "dirty and germ ridden"— delivered by emotional "victims"—would be devastating.

Their strategy was twofold. First, the hospital held an educational press briefing in collaboration with a nonprofit health organization explaining that staph infections are a global health problem and that, thankfully, the hospital was leading the effort to address it locally. The outside experts explained that the spread of staph is caused in large part by the public bringing the nasty germ *into* the hospitals. Soon thereafter, hospital-sponsored educational materials and public service advertisements conveyed to the community that fighting staph is a shared responsibility (not just the duty of one hospital), and that hand washing and the proper use of antibiotics (not lawsuits) are the best defense. The hospital had deftly shifted from defense to offense.

Thus step one preempted the allegations and framed the issue. Step two was to go right at the opposition via a second press conference specific to the lawsuits. Through advance planning and the constant monitoring of the courthouse, the hospital was able to assemble the media within minutes of the lawsuits being filed to get its side of the story out first, *before* the plaintiffs could even announce their allegations. The hospital's leadership, supported by independent experts on hospital germ control, denounced the lawsuits as factually wrong, reckless, and irresponsible, and, if successful, potentially very injurious to the hospital's ability to provide adequate care to the community. Guess whose sound bites—and story—led the evening news? By playing offense, the hospital had denied the other side the ability to attack first and frame the issue.

CHANGING THE DEBATE

Consumer product companies tend to be very reluctant issue warriors. They are slow to defend and rarely go on the offensive. But when one consumer goods company found its flagship product—a household cleaner—on the verge of being eliminated from the marketplace, its backbone stiffened considerably.

The challenge was that the cleaner's active ingredient released tiny, truly inconsequential amounts of chemical residues, which tests showed were safe at low levels. Initially, the company had, in effect, pleaded to regulators, "Hey, our wonderful product only pollutes in parts per trillion." To which officials responded along the lines of, "The law is the law—so reformulate!" Reformulation would have gutted the product's efficacy and essentially spelled the end for this important category leader.

In response, their new strategy was to turn an environmental issue into a food-safety issue. Since the product was effective at killing *E. coli,* salmonella, and other dangerous food-borne contagions, the company mobilized food safety and health groups concerned about food-borne disease. Doctors from hospitals where the product was used as a disinfectant were also asked to express concern that an invaluable tool in the fight against deadly bacteria was about to be forced from supermarket shelves. Press conferences, grassroots communications, editorials, and public education materials sparked a flood of calls and letters to government officials. The emotive benefits of saving children from death and disease were far stronger than the theoretical threats of a minute, barely detectable reduction in air pollution.

As the late senator Everett Dirkson famously said, "When I feel the heat, I see the light." And so it was for these government officials. The regulation was rescinded, and legislation was soon passed granting the product a multiyear grace period.

HIGHLIGHTING HYPOCRISY

If there was any group of companies that needed to go on the offensive against its detractors, it was the biotechnology and pharmaceutical companies. During the last several years, these companies were under attack by extreme animal rights groups. Infiltrations, hidden cameras, threats, intimidation, vandalism, and protests were just some of the tactics employed. Another was the use of misguided movie and television stars to raise money, generate press interest, and mainstream the cause. But when a chance emerged to turn the tables, one tough-minded public education group, the Foundation for Biomedical Research (FBR), did just that.

The opportunity arose at the height of AIDS activism during the late 1990s, when a few Hollywood celebrities, including Alec Baldwin and his wife, Kim Basinger, made a point of wearing the red AIDS ribbon—the symbol of support for AIDS research—at various public functions and publicity stops. They presented themselves as champions of a cure for this horrible disease.

There was just one problem. These celebrities and a handful of others were also very public supporters of People for the Ethical Treatment of Animals (PETA), the radical animal rights group whose president, Ingrid Newkirk, stated that "even if animal research meant a cure for AIDS, I'd be against it." To be sure, if the scientific and medical community were to actually be denied animal testing, not only would AIDS research virtually grind to a stop, there would be little way of knowing if any new therapies were safe and effective. A touch hypocritical, don't you think, to be leading the call for new AIDS medicines at one venue while accepting an award at another from a group that works extremely aggressively to block AIDS research?

FBR went on the offensive. It released a stinging report, "Hype & Hypocrisy," that detailed the cynical—or, at minimum, thoughtless—words and deeds of those celebrities who simultaneously promote medical research and an animal rights movement that actively thwarts it. National media coverage was immediate and highly supportive. The headline of *USA Today*'s article was clear enough: "Report: Medical Coverage Impeded." The *Washington Post*'s front-page story "Cause Celebre Conflict, It's Animal Rights vs. AIDS Research" also drew heavily from what FBR had uncovered. Hollywood actors no longer could claim the moral high ground in lecturing scientists, patients, and pharmaceutical companies about the evils of animal research, at least if they expected to have any credibility as AIDS activists.

SHOWCASING BENEFITS TO BALANCE THE SCORECARD

Playing offense can take a variety of different forms. It needn't always require going after one's adversaries. It can mean simply putting your best foot forward. The plastics industry's response to rising environmental concerns in the 1990s is a good case in point. At the time it was called "the solid waste crisis," and the overhyped premise was that America was running out of landfill space and unless something draconian was done, we'd be up to our eyes in trash. It all came to a head when the media seized on the story of a New York City "garbage barge" traveling up and down the Eastern seaboard looking for a taker for its load of trash. It never found one.

But the issue was serious. Spurred by these media reports and pressure from environmental groups, legislatures at all levels of government were threatening plastics manufacturers with demands to either eliminate their use in packaging altogether, or to set recycling standards so high that no one could use the material.

The industry responded first and foremost with product reformulation and redesign, and by openly supporting recycling programs and facilities. But it also went on the offensive in trying to win over public opinion. After extensive consumer research and message testing, it launched a very well-funded national campaign, dubbed "Plastics Make It Possible," to remind people of the many food safety, medical, and public health benefits of plastics. It drove up the product's benefits and raised awareness of the downsides of eliminating the material, and led to a more reasonable middle ground to addressing solid waste issues.

There is a maxim in politics that if you're explaining, you're losing. Companies in trouble need to do the right thing, but sometimes that includes going on the offense, whether that means pushing back at detractors or simply reminding people why you're worth supporting in the first place.

CHAPTER 5

Cloak Every Argument in a Principle

But you can't hold a whole fraternity responsible for the behavior of a few sick, twisted individuals. For if you do, then, shouldn't we blame the whole fraternity system? And if the whole fraternity system is guilty, then isn't this an indictment of our educational institutions in general? I put it to you, Greg, isn't this an indictment of our entire American society? Well, you can do whatever you want to us, but we're not going to sit here and listen to you bad-mouth the United States of America!

—OTTER, *ANIMAL HOUSE*

Ronald Reagan once advised, "Wrap every argument in a principle." And every effective communicator must know how to do it. Essentially, it means taking an issue, position, or call-to-action and associating it with a timeless value—something most people cherish or hold sacrosanct. Security. Justice. Privacy. Choice. Safety. The rights of the underprivileged. Fighting oppression. Doing so adds enormous authority and weight to one's claim. You're not just espousing a selfish point of view; you're standing up for something noble. Not only does it win people over to your side, it enables them to justify their position to others.

Furthermore, never overestimate the public's true interest in your issue or the intellectual energy they will commit to sifting through competing facts before making a judgment. Most public opinion researchers agree that the average American is "smart but ignorant." They are bright. And they know what they know—which is quite a lot about *their* job, *their* profession, *their* family, *their* hobbies, etc. But don't expect them to know much about *your* company, *your* products, and *your* issues. For communicators this means if you can't convince people in 30 seconds, you're not going to.

TELLING CONSUMERS WHY THEY SHOULD CARE

Take, for example, the classic marketplace slugfest between the telephone companies and the cable television industry. For years, they have competed for access to the vast and always evolving TV-Internet-digital consumer market. Beginning in the mid-1980s, Congress has intervened to referee where and how these two goliath industries can wire their way into U.S. households—sometimes called the fight for "the last mile"—and under what terms. Once politicians are involved, the race is on to persuade the public to pick sides and pressure their elected representatives.

US Telecom, the trade association representing Verizon, BellSouth, AT&T, and other telecommunications companies, isn't subtle about what principles it's basing its PR campaign on. Its advertising theme is: "TV FREEDOM. Freedom to choose. Freedom to save." The ads are optimistic and empowering. The word "choice" is used a lot. The message is very clear: Our side is about giving consumers precisely what they want, versus the one-size-fits-all approach of cable companies.

The National Cable Trade Association (NCTA), on the other hand, avoids the consumer choice argument and tries to persuade legislators via the venerable "jobs, jobs, jobs" appeal. It associates itself with Main Street America through folksy, small-town imagery. Its advertising copy reads: "John West was laid off, twins on the way. Cable offered John a fresh start. Cable kept its commitment to America, while other industries folded or outsourced." A tagline presents the cable industry as "A Great American Success Story." This message is more purely political: Mr. Congressman, do not forget we're the industry (not the big telecoms) that's providing jobs in your home district!

To be fair, the cable ads are politically powerful and they try hard to connect emotionally. Yet they almost concede, from a consumer standpoint, that cable doesn't have any competitive advantage over its telecom competition. They need to respond to US Telecom's claim of consumer superiority by stressing reliability, cost, service, or content. They need to counterattack. In the long run, most members of Congress will support the industry they think the public wants, not the one that appears the most patriotic, even if it does create jobs for folks back home. In any event, this battle for the moral high ground is sure to go several more rounds. Stay tuned to see whether US Telecom's "freedom and choice" can trump NCTA's "We've got a job for your unemployed brother-in-law."

BECOMING ONE OF THE "GOOD GUYS"

Science-based industries in particular have been remiss in communicating in resonant, emotional terms, hoping instead that "the facts" will win over skeptical audiences. One case in point is the food-biotechnology sector, which has struggled for years to find a way to convince consumers that their genetically modified crops are a net positive for the world. At first blush, the technology's benefits appear very persuasive. Tests show these enhanced plants are resistant to drought, disease, and ravenous insects; promise increased yields under harsh growing conditions; and sometimes require fewer pesticides and other chemical inputs.

Yet antibiotech activists, environmentalists, and progressive farm groups have raised enough theoretical concerns—and manufactured sufficient media controversy—to impede the introduction of some of these products and to entirely block others in Europe and elsewhere.

A big part of the challenge has been that most of the early product applications were great for farmers (enabling greater production at less cost) but delivered very little in terms of a clear consumer benefit, such as cheaper prices, improved taste, or better nutrition. But, after a decade of unabated controversy, especially in protectionist Europe, biotech champions at last discovered a compelling moral high ground: starving Africans. True, Africa didn't represent much of a commercial market. However, the greater ability of these more resilient genetically modified crops to withstand the continent's tough growing conditions was enthusiastically welcomed by struggling African farmers and rural development leaders.

Critics of genetically modified crops soon discovered it is

one thing to stir up concern over the sale of "Frankenfoods" in the affluent cities of Europe and America, and quite another to be seen as denying impoverished Africans the agriculture tools they need to feed their townships.

The tide started to turn when former president Jimmy Carter (not known for his support of big business) got on the bandwagon. In a rare departure from his environmentalist loyalties, he publicly endorsed the use of biotechnology-enhanced crops, especially in developing nations. He argued that the proven benefits of this technology to people in need far outweigh the theoretical risks. Today Europe remains stubbornly opposed to these promising new foods, and, having been excluded from the organic club, biotech foods still face stiff PR challenges in the United States. But this PR-troubled industry has found a moral high ground, and that's a start.

Far more sure-footed at this game are U.S. gun owners and agriculture interests. The National Rifle Association (NRA) has for decades repelled nearly every government attempt to restrict access to firearms, in large part by evoking the Second Amendment to the Constitution, which states, "A well regulated Militia, being necessary to the security of a free State, the right of the people to keep and bear Arms, shall not be infringed." Legal scholars and concerned citizens on both sides will debate to eternity the relevancy of this passage to the contemporary challenges of reducing violence via handguns. But what is certain is that the NRA will not only fight any restrictions on their merits, it will claim the moral high ground of a Constitutional amendment in support of its position.

Over the last 60 years, the number of Americans who make their living off the land has steadily plunged, and many farms have assumed the scale of a midsized manufacturing plant. Yet politically they are as powerful as ever—at least if their access to billions in federal farming subsidies is the measurement. Their power lies in the fact that simply by being farmers they own the moral high ground. It takes a brave—or foolish—politician to get on the wrong side of a constituency whose image as earnest, hardworking, honest folk has been forged by two hundred years of American rural mythology.

Claiming the moral high ground needn't be reserved just for managing crises and lobbying politicians. Some companies have built their entire business model around being perceived as business Good Guys—none more self-consciously than ice cream icon Ben & Jerry's. Through a mix of folksy marketing and progressive moralizing, the company has won over a public nostalgic for the Flower Power '60s while inoculating itself against a host of nutritional, food safety, and environmental complaints directed at its more conventional competition. Heart disease is America's number one killer, but who can blame two bearded guys running a business in sandals?

This isn't to suggest that Ben & Jerry's hasn't lived up to its values, or that these aren't well conceived. It clearly put a lot of thought and energy into "the right way of doing business" and is smart enough to back it up. The point here for crisis managers is that by cultivating a moral high ground position—and promoting it through pop-cultural imagery—the company has signaled to the news media and activists that it would be more publicly saleable to blame some other company (e.g., McDonald's) for clogged arteries and overweight kids.

While it is relatively easy to make people feel good about farmers and ice cream merchants, the going gets rougher when the industry in question has a terminally bad public image, like big oil and drug companies. At first blush, the moral high ground message for pharmaceutical companies would seem a no-brainer: Our products save your lives! Over the past decade, easily over a billion dollars have been poured into TV and print ads (and PR campaigns) by these companies and their trade associations to convey just this idea. They stress in one way or another that Aunt Sally's diabetes, Grandpa's arthritis, or your sister's breast cancer is cured or under control thanks to Big Pharma. And it's all true! But these ads completely miss the point.

The problem isn't that people don't appreciate medicine. It's that everyone thinks it costs too much. For better or worse, the public believes that world-class health care is a right and an entitlement. And when they are told that these same companies are making "obscene profits" while their own health care costs are spiraling out of control, it sends them over the edge. While the public is saying, "We love your products but we're having a big problem affording them," the drug companies keep saying back, "Please like us because Billy can walk again."

Everyone gets the medical miracles part; it's the cost part that needs some serious communications work. GlaxoSmith-Kline finally got it right when it launched a straight-talk advertising and PR campaign in 2004 that provided the American public with frank, on-point information about drug development, drug costs, and drug safety. Unfortunately, it has been too little too late. Claiming the moral high ground doesn't work if you're perceived as avoiding the real issues.

IT'S NOT EASY BEING GREEN

Faced with an equally angry and cynical public, British Petroleum has taken a polar opposite approach. As a giant oil company during a time when energy prices are sky high and environmental concerns about global warming border on fanaticism, BP has surrendered any pretense of claiming a moral high ground. For the most part, its print, transit, and television ads deemphasize the company's core business (oil exploration and refining) while highlighting its alternative-energy investments as well as its efforts to reduce pollution. Unlike the drug makers, BP addresses the industry's negatives—in this case, pollution—head-on and presents the steps both the company and consumers can take to do something about them. "It's a Start," the campaign's tagline humbly suggests. British Petroleum is transformed to Beyond Petroleum. The new company logo is a sunflower.

Where the ads presumably succeed is in connecting with younger, hip, primarily urban audiences, and in giving BP a voice that, like Ben & Jerry's, is nonthreatening and self-consciously "uncorporate." This makes good sense. Today big oil companies are regarded not just cynically but with outright hostility by large numbers of consumers, and the ad campaign succeeds at cutting through those communications barriers. There is little question that BP, through this creative and groundbreaking campaign, has strongly differentiated itself from other Big Oil producers and, perhaps, carved out a new segment of supporters. Bravo for that!

But is BP truly advancing a thoughtful energy debate or simply buying time with its critics? Even if alternative energy succeeds beyond the experts' wildest expectations, the environmentally stressful and occasionally sloppy work of digging for more crude oil must continue for decades. Will the public and its most vocal critics feel betrayed if, years from now, BP hasn't really gotten beyond petroleum after all? Has BP been too clever for its own good? Time will tell.

Moreover, when BP encountered a series of severe crises and controversies in 2005–2006, ranging from allegations of commodity-trading fraud to a leaky Alaskan oil line, it quickly became clear that feel-good advertising does not create a "trust bank" that can be drawn from when the going gets rough. The lesson here is that while there is much to be gained by BP's bold, direct approach to public dialogue, blanketing a giant oil company in flower petals can come back to bite you when the oily realities of a pipeline leak hit the front pages.

One of the most common genres of allegations facing business is product safety, as in a lack thereof. Makers of cars, drugs, toys, appliances, cosmetics, foods, and beverages, among many others, all have been hit hard by charges of danger or risk. More recently, industry critics have evoked a concept called the Precautionary Principle, in essence a "better safe than sorry" argument that is seductive in its commonsense appeal but, when applied in the extreme, can eliminate safe products from the marketplace.

In those situations, the best moral high ground is consumer choice—the right for consumers to decide for themselves, as responsible adults, what products they use. Consumer choice is empowerment. It is independence. It is freedom from the elitist heavy hand of the "nanny culture" that aspires to run our lives. Evoking consumer choice turns the tables on self-appointed industry watchdogs. They are quick to lay claim to the role of consumer advocate, but what better advocate than consumers themselves? Of course, leveraging the power of consumer choice also requires information, so that consumers are fully advised of real risks and provided the facts they need to make well-informed decisions.

For example, we have come to accept that prescription and over-the-counter drugs come with all sorts of warnings. Consumers can decide for themselves whether those risks are acceptable. Critics eager to eliminate or restrict access to many of our most popular foods—soft drinks and the like—have a rougher go of it because these products' labels are chock-full of caloric and nutritional information. So it's not that consumers are gaining weight because they don't know what they're eating. While warnings and product label information should never be frivolous, too many companies fight them and end up paying the price.

WINDY POLITICIANS SHOW THE WAY

Sometimes, claiming the moral high ground requires a large dose of creativity, especially when the whiff of hypocrisy is in the air. Take the case of Senator Edward "Ted" Kennedy, Democrat from Massachusetts, and his bout with a floating "wind farm" development planned for the coastal waters of Nantucket Sound right by his Hyannis Port compound. Reportedly, he was none too pleased when he learned that the project would consist of 130 very tall turbines—many within plain sight of the fabled summer home he once shared with his late great parents and siblings. And, frankly, who can blame him? Not many of us would want to look out from our deck at 24 miles of spinning windmills!

But, there was just one problem for the senator. The other side had an imposing claim to the moral high ground, too. Aesthetics aside, the huge upside of this massive project was it would generate enough pollution-free power for 124,000 local homes. Moreover, Kennedy has a 40-year track record in the Senate as an unfailing environmentalist, and all the big green groups supported the windmill project. If alternative energy is something that everyone supports in theory, at some point you have to step up and support it in reality. And, come to think of it, who wants to look like a rich hypocrite? Realizing that just coming right out and saying "I'm Ted Kennedy, damn it, and I don't want a clattering collection of spinning hardware ruining my ocean view" was not the wisest of approaches, his handlers toiled, really toiled, to find . . . the moral high ground.

"[The project] is a giveaway of public land that belongs to the country," the senator asserted. "Those credits are coming from *working families.*" Bingo! Instead of this simply being another case of "I'm all for giant windmills as long as they're not near my vacation home," Mr. Kennedy positioned this as another case of the good senator standing up for the Little Guy.

So, whatever you are promoting or defending, victory often goes to the side claiming the moral high ground. Wrapping your argument in a principle resonates with a power that a sterile recitation of the facts can never match. But the claim has got to be credible and delivered with a gut feel for how much spin the public can withstand.

CHAPTER 6

Preach to the Choir

Appeasement is the policy of feeding the alligator in hopes
you will be the last to be eaten.

—WINSTON CHURCHILL

There were two types of people at the conference at the
exclusive CEO retreat: people who run the world, and
people who advised them. We advisors were there to brief Information Age billionaires and corporate titans—and the occasional royal family member—about our areas of expertise, which
ranged from venture capital to crisis management.

We entered the conference with a fundamental misconcep-
tion: We expected that the great powers in attendance would be
concerned about the wave of anticorporate sentiment sweeping
the globe, and about fending off their critics. We were only half
right.

While these elites were indeed upset about the growing
hostility toward multinational companies, the vast majority of
them were interested in cultivating their adversaries—winning

over the people who despise them. The instinct to make peace with one's adversaries is understandable; however, we sensed a more disturbing phenomenon at work. When we raised the option of reaching out to media and policy leaders who were sympathetic to free markets and globalization, most of them turned up their noses. These industry elites preferred to focus on winning over the very people and institutions that were devoted to their destruction.

We queried the attendees about their financial contributions, and were astonished to find that the majority gave large sums of money to organizations that routinely attacked them:

> "Why do you give money to people who hate you?"
> "We need to have a dialogue with these groups, keep a line of communication open."
> "But they *still* attack you."

The discussion ended there, such was the commitment of these business leaders to support their adversaries.

The latest rage in public relations is "building bridges" between corporations and their ideological adversaries. Occasionally, these arrangements make sense because there are times when accommodations can be reached. In many crises and marketplace assaults, however, there are inherent conflicts between opposing camps that are irreconcilable.

One of the greatest myths of public relations is that you can get hostile audiences to like you. In reality, you can only "spin" a public that *wants* to be spun—reinforcing existing sentiments and prejudices, rather than reversing fundamental positions.

The term "spin doctor" first surfaced in the early 1980s. It was used primarily by Democrats to explain the success of President Ronald Reagan's White House. *The public doesn't actually like Reagan*, was the implication; *they're being fooled against their will by clever propagandists*. During the Clinton years, Republicans, outraged by President Clinton's capacity to withstand criticism, returned the favor, attributing his success to something inauthentic—spin, jive, personified by Clinton advisor James Carville.

In reality, nobody was fooled. Both presidents just kept doing what they did best, which was to leverage their strong personalities with audiences who were already inclined to support them.

We've seen delusions of value-changing propaganda at work in our current war on terror. Many pundits have speculated on what we can do to stop Islamic fundamentalists from hating us. While over a long period of time moderate Muslims may become attracted to Western culture—and this should be encouraged—never in the history of wartime propaganda has it been the goal to get your enemy to like you. Rather, the chief objective of wartime communications is to rally one's allies and frighten one's enemies.

Nevertheless, utopian thinking prevails in many boardrooms. We were once meeting with the management of a company that was under attack for allegedly making unsafe products. We showed them a PowerPoint presentation that contained a list of special interests aligned against them, along with their adversaries' estimated budgets.

"Where are these people getting all of this money to attack us?" the CEO asked.

"In part, from you," we answered.

The meeting became uncomfortable as we explained how his own company had been contributing to the organizations that had been attacking them, yet he balked at spending a fraction of that amount to defend his company, concerned that any such activity would further provoke those whom another branch of his company was hoping to cultivate.

The phrase "preach to the choir" has a negative connotation. It suggests a useless endeavor, a waste of time. In a crisis management or marketplace assault, nothing could be further from the truth. Some of the most successful communications defenses involve rallying one's base, even if it means provoking one's adversaries.

When seven-time Tour de France winner Lance Armstrong was accused of using performance-enhancing drugs by French officials, he did not plead with them to change their position. He strongly condemned their methods but focused his energies where it mattered—on his fans and commercial supporters.

Plaintiffs' lawyers have made fortunes and dominated the political landscape by supporting elected officials and policy groups that agree with them. Not only do plaintiffs' lawyers not seek to "build bridges" with their critics, they openly attack them.

DISPOSABLE DIAPERS AND THE BOTTOM LINE ABOUT GRASSROOTS SUPPORT

In the late 1980s and early 1990s, disposable diapers began to draw criticism because they create more solid waste. There was a temporary landfill shortage, and the news was replete with reports about a wandering garbage barge that lacked a destination and Americans being buried alive in our own garbage.

Some legislatures were even proposing taxes and bans on disposable diapers, suggesting that they were uniquely responsible for clogging landfills. During this time, we worked for a coalition of disposable diaper manufacturers. Our opinion research on the subject turned up intense support for the product by parents of young children. However, those whose households did not use disposable diapers were more willing to tax and ban them. Self-interest ruled the debate as usual.

Those who most vehemently resented the prospect of punitive actions against diapers were working mothers. In a focus group, one mother said, "The minute we get a product that makes our lives easier, somebody wants to ban it." The intensity of the statement was palpable. The very same mothers who spoke lovingly about their children directed their fury toward the faceless enemy, "Somebody."

The battle over disposable diapers evolved into a women's rights issue, and while Hollywood celebrities were touting the virtues of cloth diapers, show business types had the luxury of servants who could deal with the mess associated with cloth. Working mothers became resentful that a product that was sanitary and convenient was under attack by a (perceived) elite class—increasingly celebrities and college-age environmentalists who didn't have children.

Disposable diaper industry communications were then focused almost exclusively on working mothers, the objective being to create "permission" to keep using disposables—and "permission" to be politically outraged that an elite was seeking to deprive them of a product they valued. The industry educated the "choir" of working mothers about the extraordinary progress that had been made in creating smaller and thinner diapers and in reducing waste at every stage of the product's life cycle. Recycled content from plastic milk jugs were introduced into plastic diaper packaging. Studies were commissioned comparing the air pollution caused by washing cloth diapers with the solid waste consequences of disposable diapers. The net message: No diaper is environmentally consequence-free, so you might as well stick with the product that works better.

The legislators who proposed punitive actions against disposable diapers found themselves lined up against citizens who voted. At the height of the controversy, NBC's *Today Show*'s Jane Pauley, a mother of four, questioned an antidiaper activist on the air. The line of questioning was less about the environmental aspects of disposable diapers than whether the antidiaper crusader was a mother. She wasn't, a point that was not lost on the viewers. Pauley's nonverbal cues conveyed the ridicule of millions of parents.

The taxes and bans that had been proposed in legislatures failed. The cloth diaper fad swiftly ended, proving a colossal and expensive inconvenience. Major diaper manufacturers kept introducing thinner, lighter disposables. The scare du jour—being buried alive in garbage—evaporated as attention turned to an emerging recession.

Throughout the attack on disposable diapers, the target of communications was consumers who already believed in—and needed—the product. There would have been no benefit to reaching out to audiences that had no investment in the product on the grounds that "educating" them would benefit the overall campaign. The triumph of disposable diapers was tied directly to the efficacy of the product and the loyalty to a concentrated community that the diapers inspired.

One of the first tactics that surfaces after a corporate crisis breaks out is an image advertisement. The ad inevitably features smiling employees, perhaps children, and professions of deep commitment to consumers and other offended parties. Do ads like this really work?

It depends on who the audience is believed to be. Our experience has been that image advertisements do very little to move the opinions of people who hold deep prejudices against the company. However, audiences that already have a vested interest in the company—employees, customers, shareholders—are greatly affected by such advertisements because they want to see that their company is in the fight.

We counsel clients to run ads like this specifically for the purpose of preaching to the choir because in a crisis, these people are your "base," the ones with the greatest incentive to support you when many others won't.

The same rule that applies to image advertisements applies to crisis management. Dispense with the fantasy that one's natural enemies can somehow be persuaded to come over to your side. Immediately pursue natural allies who can be mobilized on your behalf on a moment's notice. "Wish lists" of allies (every health care company under fire wants former surgeon general C. Everett Koop to speak out for them) and potential consumer-group spokespersons lend an appearance of strategic fullness to crisis management plans but seldom pan out in real-world situations.

When under attack, the perfect spokesperson should not be the enemy of the good. A doctor from a state university is more preferable in defending, say, a pharmaceutical product on *Good Morning America* than a Nobel laureate who theoretically supports your position but who isn't available in a pinch.

The choir may not comprise everyone you want, but it may comprise everyone you've actually got. And that's a more valuable asset to your company than you might realize.

CHAPTER 7

Damage Control Means More Than Having to Say You're Sorry

When they invented "I'm sorry," honor was lost.

—GREEK PROVERB

The most common question a crisis manager gets at a barbecue: "Why don't your clients just fess up and apologize?" The question is often smugly followed by, "If Nixon had just admitted 'I screwed up' and said he was sorry, the whole thing would have blown over. . . ."

Wrong. Instead of resigning and rising off into the heavens on Marine One in anticipation of a pardon, Nixon would probably have been tried in a court of law, convicted, and dragged down Pennsylvania Avenue chained to a pickup truck.

The scandal-plagued refuse to apologize because they don't think they're guilty. Sometimes they're not. Guilty or innocent, a protective enzyme kicks in that creates a barrier between one's actions and one's self-perception. No matter how wicked an individual or institution is, what's universal is the desire to be loved and respected independent of one's actions.

―――――

But a more strategic reason clients in crisis don't "fess up" is because it's often a very bad idea.

Crises have legal implications. Despite pretrial cries for Martha Stewart to apologize for her involvement in her alleged insider trading scandal, she couldn't, because in a court of law, an apology may be interpreted by a judge and jury as an admission of guilt. One cannot, after all, apologize for what one did not do. This logic applies to civil litigation as much as it does to criminal trials, which is why we see so few corporate apologies.

The tension between legal and public relations considerations should be adjudicated by the answer to one question: Would you rather be loved or acquitted? If the latter is the answer, silence is golden—especially for corporations, which are almost always seen as being guilty, not to mention irredeemable.

The apology has its practical origins in ancient Greek culture. When Plato issued his "Apologia" on behalf of Socrates, he was offering a defense, not suggesting Socrates was sorry for anything.

The mission of the apology shifted with the rise of Christianity, where winning God's love and forgiveness became the goal. In order for one to restore one's self to God's grace, one needed to convey remorse and sustain a punishment of some kind in order to demonstrate that a valuable lesson had been learned. Reparations then needed to be made to the injured parties, to God. In Catholicism particularly, confessions occur privately with a cleric, so it's possible that one can return to God's good graces without a media advisor.

Not so in the court of public opinion. Public apologies can

come at a very high price, such as when former New Jersey governor James McGreevey announced in 2004 that he was gay and then resigned when allegations surfaced that he had appointed a purported love interest to a government job. The good news was that the story quickly evaporated. The bad news was that McGreevey was out of a job.

THE TRANSACTIONAL APOLOGY

In crisis management, an apology is a transaction whereby the accused humbles himself in exchange for mercy. It is offered as a gesture marking the end of the play, the final encore permitting the audience to go home, the turning of the proverbial page so that a new chapter can begin. It most certainly does not necessarily equate with repentance or sorrow.

The contemporary apology is cheap. Everybody's doing it, from presidents to deranged ear-chomping prizefighters. The apology is the tactic du jour of the public relations industry because it is seen as a way for the mighty to show human qualities. The apology often stops short of confession, employing weasel words that give the apologizer immunity from the consequences of the original sin.

The key question is "Do apologies *work* as a crisis management technique?" An apology "works" when a transaction occurs whereby something small is surrendered (pride) but something of value—such as one's freedom—is preserved.

Transactional apologies can be effective, but there's a catch: The *carrot* of apology works best when accompanied by the *stick* of personal exposure for the adversary.

Take the case of Los Angeles Lakers basketball star Kobe

Bryant, who was accused of raping a nineteen-year-old woman who worked at the front desk of a Colorado hotel in June 2003. A few weeks later, Bryant appeared at a news conference with his wife and admitted to adultery but denied rape. In the months that followed, Bryant's accuser was publicly identified, and allegations about her supposedly active sex life and emotional instability surfaced on the Internet and in the news media. These reports, which presumably weren't discouraged by Bryant's attorneys, included a drug overdose, suicide attempts, drug rehabilitations, bipolar disorder, showing up at a rape clinic with underwear containing semen from several men, and, perhaps most damningly, an audition for *American Idol* suggesting a penchant for self-dramatizing publicity.

In September 2004, with jury selection under way, the case against Bryant was dismissed when his accuser decided not to testify. Bryant publicly stated:

> Although I truly believe this encounter between us was consensual, I recognize now that she did not and does not view the incident the same way I did. After months of reviewing discovery, listening to her attorney and even her testimony in person, I now understand how she feels she did not consent to this encounter.

Some found the combination of the Bryant team's tactics with his "nonapology" reprehensible. Perhaps, but this carrot-and-stick approach helped Bryant dodge a grueling trial that may have resulted in four years to life in the slammer and cost him blue-chip corporate endorsements. Instead, he resumed his $136 million Lakers contract.

SIN AND SYMPATHY IN THE CLINTON WARS

Like Kobe Bryant, President Bill Clinton combined the carrot of repentant gestures with the stick of simultaneously savaging his critics, actually gaining momentum from ad hominem criticism.

During the 1992 presidential campaign, Clinton's national name recognition polled at 5 percent until *60 Minutes* decided to explore his alleged affair with lounge singer Gennifer Flowers. Bill and Hillary Clinton went on the program, and the Arkansas governor admitted to "causing pain" in his marriage. This was neither an admission of nor an apology for adultery, but it worked. Clinton's name recognition shot up to 90 percent after the show aired.

Clinton's ability to convert sin into sympathy didn't stop there. On January 21, 1998, the story about Clinton's affair with intern Monica Lewinsky broke in the mainstream media. With his job approval rating at 55 percent, and under searing pressure to address the controversy, Clinton uttered his infamous denial on January 26, "I did not have sexual relations with that woman, Miss Lewinsky." This was, of course, a lie. The following day, a poll was conducted following Clinton's State of the Union address, placing his job approval rating at 73 percent!

As the facts of the Lewinsky affair continued to trickle out, Clinton undertook spiritual outreach, including sessions with the Reverend Jesse Jackson and revival-style prayer sessions at African-American churches. Operatives loyal to Clinton also got to work on his adversaries.

On October 4, 1998, publisher Larry Flynt placed an advertisement in the *Washington Post* offering "up to a million dollars" to anyone who could demonstrate proof of Republican hypocrisy in the effort to impeach Clinton over a sex scandal. *New York Times* columnist Maureen Dowd said of the ad, "Flynt is clearly looking for a deliciously high duplicity level. . . . We [need] a real shocker." The Republicans' worst nightmare came when Flynt retained investigative reporter Dan E. Moldea, who had . been standing up to Mafia kingpins, assassins, and corrupt union bosses for decades. Moldea, who made no bones about sympathizing with President Clinton's struggle, proceeded to systematically expose the sex lives of Republican congressional leaders on the grounds that they were not qualified to judge Clinton's morality. Regardless of where one stands on the political spectrum and the techniques employed on both sides of the Clinton wars, one thing soon became clear: The strategy worked.

In the months that followed, House Speaker Newt Gingrich was hammered in the press about his extramarital affairs. His designated successor, House Judiciary Committee chairman Henry Hyde, was forced to answer questions about a long-ago extramarital affair as he was preparing articles of impeachment against Clinton. Congressman Robert Livingston, Gingrich's would-be successor as Speaker, stepped aside on December 19, 1998, when his own related troubles surfaced on the day of Clinton's impeachment. All of these things—considered fair game by the news media—made Clinton's foibles appear to be less shameful.

Theories about Clinton's popularity corresponded with one's politics and worldview. Lying works, some concluded; after all, Clinton did better when prevaricating than when he told the truth and apologized. His August 17, 1998, apology for lying to the nation was universally condemned as a disaster, but his poll numbers took a hop to above 70 percent shortly after he was impeached in the House of Representatives and acquitted in the Senate. By the time the scandal was long behind him, an October 21, 1999, poll showed that 77 percent of the American public declared Clinton's presidency a success.

There was something in the interplay of President Clinton's charismatic-yet-vulnerable personality and his times that made him uniquely able to benefit from adversity. Cues of victimization pay dividends only if your audience likes you in the first place. The women's rights movement, which had crusaded against sexual harassment in the workplace in the years leading up to the Lewinsky drama—and which should have theoretically been most offended by Clinton's behavior—was conspicuously absent in his excoriation. The reason: Some combination of liking him personally and supporting his policies.

Making one's adversaries appear worse by comparison makes for an effective accompaniment if you've got something on your adversary that's considered relevant. No matter how many times Republican leaders said "It's about lying, not sex," a majority of Americans felt "it" *was* about sex, which is why the scorched-earth tactics against Republican leaders worked. And Bill Clinton prospered.

WHY THREE APOLOGIES DON'T ADD UP TO FORGIVENESS

On January 14, 2005, Harvard University president Lawrence Summers spoke at a conference on women in science. He was under the impression that his remarks would be off the record. This was his first mistake. His second was choosing as his subject speculation on how biological differences between men and women might account for why women aren't more successful in math and science. Outrage broke out on campus.

In a letter posted on Harvard's Web site several days later, Summers wrote, "I deeply regret the impact of my comments and apologize for having not weighed them more carefully. . . . I was wrong to have spoken in a way that was an unintended signal of discouragement to talented girls and women." Summers apologized three different times.

He wasn't forgiven.

Pointing out biological differences has a certain Third Reich whiff about it. Saying, for example, that blacks predominate in athletics is perceived as a backhanded way of saying (wink, wink), "they" aren't as smart scholastically. Saying that women are weaker in math and science validates the stereotype that women are emotional (read: not rational).

Despite his contrition, Summers didn't fare as well with women in his ordeal as his former boss, President Clinton, did during his.

Professor Harvey Mansfield believed that Summers received bad advice from Kennedy School of Government professor and political advisor David Gergen: "He said if you apologize, you'll make yourself look weak and vulnerable, and women will feel sympathetic. . . . He took that advice and, of course, the women despised him for looking weak, just as men would have done. So his backpedaling was a big mistake and hasn't been successful. . . ."

Indeed, one of the great mirages of crisis management is the notion that an apology will lead to catharsis, the sense of relief associated with absolution. The problem is that human affairs are not static, they are dynamic, with an ever-shifting cast of characters and agendas vying for dominance.

In Summers's case, his apology served to validate, not neutralize, the hard nugget that lay at the core of an acute cultural conflict. In an age where agendas have multiple media in which to play out at lightning speed, Summers's original sin became a political football, forever in play.

Simple mistakes often are forgiven with an apology. Ideological shibboleths related to gender and race are not. Women in academia didn't find enough else to like about Summers and his policies to stand by him in his hour of need. Digging himself more deeply into his position wasn't a great option either, since he had already offended progressives in 2002 in a dispute with black studies professor Cornel West that drove the charismatic scholar out of Harvard to Princeton. Summers had no great options, but one thing became clear: There isn't always a correlation between apology and forgiveness. Summers announced his resignation in February 2006.

DIFFERENT OUTCOMES FOR A SIMILAR OFFENSE

Senator Trent Lott learned about the limits of apology the hard way. Why was Senator Robert Byrd (D-WV) swiftly forgiven after he apologized for his use of the word "nigger," while Lott, who used no such language, was stripped of his Senate majority leader position after a veritable apology road show for praising Strom Thurmond's political career?

The answer lies not so much in what was said as in who said it.

On March 4, 2001, Senator Byrd was speaking with Fox News's Tony Snow about improvements in race relations. During the interview, presumably in an effort to communicate that there are bad apples in all races and creeds, Byrd said:

> There are white niggers. I've seen a lot of white niggers in my time; I'm going to use that word. . . . We just need to work together to make our country a better country, and I'd just as soon quit talking about it so much.

Byrd's use of the "n-word" understandably sparked shock and outrage after the program, and Byrd quickly apologized, saying, "I apologize for the characterization I used on this program. The phrase dates back to my boyhood and has no place in today's society."

After a few frenzied days of gossip and editorializing, the subject evaporated from the news.

Senator Trent Lott's (R-MS) misadventures along racial fault lines had a very different ending. It happened in December 2002 at Strom Thurmond's 100th birthday party, when Lott said, "I want to say this about my state: When Strom Thurmond ran for president, we voted for him. We're proud of it. And if the rest of the country had followed our lead, we wouldn't have had all these problems over all these years." Thurmond's earlier career, of which Lott professed to be so fond, was anchored firmly in racial segregation.

Lott's formal apology characterized his commen
choice of words conveyed to some the impression
braced the discarded policies of the past. Nothing cou ___ ___ ___ -
ther from the truth, and I apologize to anyone who was offended
by my statement."

Some pundits claimed that Lott hadn't apologized correctly,
that he had apologized only for his statement versus the larger
ideology it conveyed. No sale: No matter how he worded his
apology, Lott was toast.

What accounts for the difference between how Byrd and Lott
were treated? Essentially this: baggage, or lack thereof. By the
time in his career that Byrd made his unfortunate remarks, he
had a decades-long history of racially progressive politics in his
portfolio. His comment, therefore, was viewed as being aberrant. One prominent African-American columnist even editori-
alized that it was hard to hold Byrd accountable for his language
when so many black people referred to each other using the vulgar term.

Apologies tend to work better when the behavior in question is viewed as aberrant versus revelatory. Lott, unlike Byrd,
had never shed his segregation-era narrative. In fact, notions of
Lott's alleged bias were validated when the press reported that
he had made almost identical remarks twenty-two years before,
when Thurmond had spoken at a campaign rally for Ronald
Reagan: "You know, if we had elected this man [Thurmond]
thirty years ago, we wouldn't be in the mess we are today."

The *Wall Street Journal* summarized Lott's abandonment by
his own party: "Lott played right into the hands of opponents

who are eager to paint the Republican Party's Southern ascendance as nothing more than old-fashioned bigotry."

Bottom line: Byrd had a job; Lott was out of a leadership position for four years—a political lifetime—until deft inside maneuvering and a very different political climate allowed him to return as senate minority whip in late 2006.

The consequences of narrative validation work on both sides of the political aisle. In 2004, CBS anchor Dan Rather apologized for a flawed *60 Minutes II* segment in which he unknowingly used forged documents to validate his thesis that President Bush received special treatment while serving in the Texas National Guard. Rather was not forgiven—and ultimately stepped down as anchor—largely because of the anti-Republican political narrative he had been cementing in broadcasting for forty years. This was a narrative that had famously included sassing an embattled President Nixon, who had asked Rather if he was "running for something" after Rather had asked a question in 1974. "No, Mr. President, are you?" Rather retorted.

In Western culture, it's understandable that we tie apology to forgiveness. This is especially tempting since the public relations industry, in a desperate attempt to win the respect of the broader culture, preaches this line so zealously. Hard evidence from the PR war zones, however, suggests that apologies work best when the violation is either aberrant or isolated. As for defusing more chronic offenses, one is more likely to be forgiven if instead of using kid gloves, one takes out the brass knuckles.

Apology Scorecard

The following are famous apologists, the allegation at issue, the damage-control action taken, and the net outcome:

President George W. Bush, 2005. Abuse of prisoners at Abu Ghraib prison in Iraq by U.S. military. Bush apologized for troops' misbehavior. Apology rejected by Arab world, but intensity of media interest dissipated with trials of abusers.

New Jersey governor James McGreevey, 2004. Appointed alleged gay lover to high office. Admitted homosexuality, apologized, and resigned. Several days of intense media coverage, interest faded, no prosecution; McGreevey returned to private life.

Baseball slugger Sammy Sosa, 2003. Used a corked bat to hit a home run, thereby raising questions about his impressive home run record. Apologized, characterized action as picking up the wrong bat by accident. Apology universally accepted due largely to Sosa's good-guy reputation.

Bicyclist Lance Armstrong, 2005. Alleged by French officials to have used performance-enhancing drugs in Tour de France. Strongly denied doping. French don't like Lance but so what? Americans do. Armstrong retired and endorsements remained lucrative.

Domestic diva Martha Stewart, 2003–2005. Convicted of lying to investigators during insider trading scandal. Denied allegations, but actively cultivated her commercial base in communications and never apologized. Convicted, went to prison, emerged with base intact, company recovered.

Catholic Church. Covered up history of molestation by priests. Stonewalled, but Vatican eventually apologized. Numerous lawsuits against the Church remain.

Coca-Cola, 1999. Tainted product made dozens ill in Europe: Coke said to be slow to respond to Belgian reports of sick schoolchildren. Recalled products in Europe, apologized to consumers. Outrage lingered overseas; Coke CEO dismissed months later.

CHAPTER 8

A Crisis Well Managed Is a Tale of Redemption

I have learned that I really cannot be destroyed.

—MARTHA STEWART

In business life, there is no better example of a successful second act than that of lifestyle mogul Martha Stewart, who was all but written off in 2003 when she was indicted for lying to investigators about her sale of ImClone stock. For the better part of two decades leading up to the debacle, Martha had solidified her position as the quintessential domestic diva who could perform big miracles with small utensils. In an era when domestic life was increasingly thought of as a corny throwback to *Ozzie & Harriet*, Martha demonstrated that a respectable working woman—a tycoon, no less—could supervise a productive household with pride. Martha wasn't just a success; her success in a way belonged to millions of women.

In the course of Martha's rise, however, something insidious happened. The women who felt that they had made Martha Stewart a success had begun to feel that they had lost control

\d become America's first self-made female
_ nad breached an altitude that made her per-
_atening, not endearing. It was one thing to cobble
_ier the perfect barbecue; it was another to be leveraging
this ability in order to fly to exotic places on private jets—places
where the rest of us couldn't go.

No one likes to believe themselves capable of resentment,
but eventually this undercurrent was detectable even in *Saturday Night Live* sketches based on Martha. It got to the point
where the big thing that was missing from Martha's American
narrative was abject humiliation. Prison nicely fit the bill. But
ironically, prison was Martha's pass, the one thing that gave us
permission to support her again. Without prison, Martha would
have been just another elitist to whom the rules did not apply.
But, whether they were an error in judgment or in character,
Martha's actions gave the public a plausible denouement: prison.
Prison took Martha from the stratosphere above us to the nether-
world beneath us.

The cliché is that "we," the public, like to build people up
and tear them down. This, however, is a one-dimensional view
that fails to capture the core feature of what we really want: a
sense of control over our icons. We want to have played a role
in making you. If we have a hand in your success, it's not a
threat because we are psychic shareholders. When that success, however, ceases to have anything to do with us, resentment
kicks in.

In court, Martha Stewart was found not guilty of stock fraud,
but she was effectively found guilty of a great metaphorical
swindle: She sold us on herself, but snatched back the shares.

She was, it turned out, just another billionaire jet-setter who got hot tips from fellow elites.

PRISON: A GOOD THING

If Martha's actions in handling her securities trading were ham-handed, her comeback maneuvers were masterful, largely because they were so realistic. Said Charles Koppelman, Stewart's wartime consigliere, "Take control of what you can control—your business."

After her indictment, Martha stepped down as CEO of her company. She worked with Koppelman to rearrange the leadership of her company, with Koppelman becoming chairman of Martha Stewart Living Omnimedia (MSLO).

When facing the choice between waiting out a potentially lengthy appeals process or going to prison sooner, Martha, in what was perhaps her boldest move, went to prison. In fact, she held a news conference to announce that she would begin her sentence as soon as she could. In crisis situations, it's often not the guilt that convicts you in the court of public opinion, it's the suspense, the not knowing what lies ahead. By putting an end to the purgatory, it allowed Martha's allies within her company and externally to get on with the planning of postprison life. "I had to do it," she said, "because I knew it would change things—jigger a change—in the company."

One of those who became attracted to Martha's plight was reality TV pioneer Mark Burnett, who proposed a show for her along the lines of Donald Trump's *The Apprentice.* Burnett, a master contemporary storyteller, found Martha's troubles to be an asset. Burnett told *Fortune,* "Donald was down too. These are winners who deal with the shit things in life. These people are inspiring."

While Stewart was in prison, the company conducted public opinion research that concluded that half the female population considered themselves to be Martha Stewart supporters. This suggested there was still a choir to preach to. It didn't really matter what those who were not Martha Stewart customers thought of her. One of the main tactics, therefore, was to create a Web site where fans could log on for updates from Martha about her life in prison and the future plans of her business.

DAMAGE-CONTROL ACTIVISM

When Martha was released from prison to spontaneous fanfare, her team opted for a controlled media approach versus a round-the-clock Marthapalooza. The problem with too much media exposure was that it would force Martha to rehash precisely the ordeal she had hoped to put behind her. Instead of live one-on-one interviews, Martha's team shot video footage of her at home with her family. A media that was thirsty for Martha news happily broadcast the choreographed footage. Martha even made the most of her six months of house arrest, hosting several thousand guests at her home during her confinement to plot her comeback.

Martha's team solidified tangible business ventures, which included her NBC "Apprentice" program, how-to DVDs from Warner Home Video based upon previously recorded shows, home entertaining musical CDs from Sony, a syndicated TV show, a satellite radio show with Sirius valued at $30 million, and a deal with a home construction company to build 650 homes, versions of Stewart's actual residences, in Martha-branded residential communities.

The future of Martha's businesses are far from certain, but her advertising revenue in Martha Stewart Living jumped 48 percent within a year of her release from prison, and the revenues of MSLO are steadily rebounding as of this writing.

A FORGIVING MARKETPLACE

Redemption is largely a tale of smallness, of vulnerability, which is why Martha Stewart, as an individual, has a better shot at it than, say, a colossus like Wal-Mart does. Wal-Mart, defined today for its singular vastness, is unlikely to return to the days when its success was admired and embodied in its crusty, pickup truck–driving founder Sam Walton. The company's current CEO could drive pickups and wear overalls twenty-four hours a day and it wouldn't neutralize the reality that the company is still known for its enormousness.

Martha Stewart's comeback happened quickly, but in reality, the best image makeovers are done quietly, over time. Coverage of President Ronald Reagan's death was striking because some of the very same reporters who despised him during his presidency claimed to like Reagan during his funeral procession. What changed? Time and the gradual demonstration of the success of his mission—namely, the destruction of Soviet communism. By winning the approval of the masses over time, he neutralized the vitriol of the elites.

Ideally, redemption evidences suffering and a demonstration of good works. Michael Milken's charitable interests, which predated his indictment for securities fraud, were not widely recognized until he served prison time, developed prostate cancer, and devoted all of his time to goodwill endeavors, a process that took a few decades to congeal. Unpopular characters and institutions can mend fences. However, rarely can this be achieved by quickie public relations stunts, which are inevitably recognized as cynical ploys.

Corporate defendants are acquitted, and personal and company crises are resolved. In 1997, sportscaster Marv Albert pleaded guilty to a misdemeanor assault charge after a mortifyingly kinky sex trial, and resumed his career as a broadcaster. Wall Street economist Lawrence Kudlow was forced to resign his lucrative job at Bear Stearns for cocaine abuse, and started over with much success as a business broadcaster on CNBC. Plenty of once-high-flying business figures have restored their lives after serious troubles, usually by addressing their problems and abiding a more modest lifestyle.

CRISIS MANAGEMENT IS ABOUT SECOND ACTS

In the Information Age, disgrace is but one of the features in a broader mosaic. There is plenty of choreography going on today, but the boundaries are wider. Whereas Gatsby was a gangster who faked being a solid citizen, today citizens are more likely to merchandise themselves as "gangstas." Whereas getting a little dirty once aced you out of country clubs, today it gives you "street cred." Scandal is nothing to aim for, but it's not the career-breaker it once was.

Against the advice of a menagerie of pundits, Martha Stewart did not "show contrition." She did not go on a road show of apology. In fact, Martha was bullheaded and vigorously fought efforts to separate her image from her company, which would have been a betrayal of shame. "If it's a brand name, you don't remove it or minimize it. It's a bad idea," she said unrepentantly—and rightly.

Martha Stewart could only be redeemed *because* she had been disgraced. The very same pundits who decried her "handling" of her indictment hailed her as a public relations genius upon her release from prison. But they missed the point. The seeds of Martha's recovery were rooted in her imprisonment. Redemption cannot occur in the absence of penance, as so many clients in crisis hope. The same public that likes to tear down the mighty were willing to let Stewart rise again once she had "cried uncle" in the form of going to prison. More than anything else, what the public wants to see is an order to the universe, that the rules still are in force. Once people have found that assurance, a reentry into the marketplace is possible.

Realism, the thing that Gatsby lacked, is what separates the survivors from the casualties. Survivors like Martha Stewart emerge from adversity understanding that their lives are different, that they will have to do things differently this time around. In order to return to the marketplace, Stewart was flexible. Despite her denials early in her scandal—denial that was largely necessary for legal reasons—she came to embrace her ordeal. Stewart became a symbol of a hardworking woman who was hyperpunished for a crime that was trivial when measured against competing scandals of the day. Her punishment was a benediction of her humanity, the very real denouement her core supporters needed to see in order to invite Stewart back into their homes.

Stewart embodies the fighting spirit, something that people sometimes publicly disdain (especially in women) but privately admire. She rejected the premise that her downfall was some kind of service to the community, or "a good thing," in her parlance.

One objective of this book is to disabuse the reader of the current dogma of surrender that permeates the public relations industry—the template that a capitalist enterprise is a guilty enterprise. To be sure, there are times when it's wise to walk away from a fight, but there are also times when one simply cannot. Tactical apologies and sensitive, new-age rhetoric should not be shibboleths of a superior morality. Assertive defenses should not be condemned as signs of immorality.

A crisis well managed is a tale of redemption. Redemption should be anchored in truth, and the best vehicle for the truth is a hearty defense—the original definition of *apologia* (not being sorry).

Martha Stewart may be many things, but one thing she is not is sorry. The very same personality trait that contributed to her initial fall, primarily her sense of destiny, was the catalyst for her redemption—the sheer self-belief that she deserved to come back. The greater the challenge confronting an individual or business, the greater sense of self the attack target must possess. The decision to get her prison sentence behind her was, in some respects, an act of defiance. "I will transcend this," was Martha's message.

Today's businesses can transcend the crises they confront, but doing so requires a belief that capitalism must be defended, not cringingly tolerated. The hackneyed chestnuts of conventional public relations have not withstood the crucible of our uniquely savage climate. When a crisis or marketplace assault hits, there is little correlation between grasping displays of good citizenship and marketplace redemption. In the future, the winners of crisis management will be the leaders of organizations who cast aside the last millennium's texts and break out an unconventional playbook fit for a drastically changed, but very rewarding, business frontier.

CHAPTER 9

When You Can't Make Them Like You, Make Them Stop Attacking You

I'm sorry we have to have a Washington presence. We thrived during our first sixteen years without any of this.

—BILL GATES, 1995

A business under sudden attack is like a human being under sudden attack. The business "feels" a simultaneous sense of shock, outrage, fear, and confusion. Presidencies and conglomerates, wrongly assumed to be unstoppable juggernauts of world domination, are reduced to hyperventilating toddlers who have lost their mothers in a crowded shopping mall.

Crisis management is about picking the best of your bad options. Sometimes "looking good"—getting a better image—is not a possibility. If public relations is about making things look good, crisis management is about making them less bad.

As the new millennium finds its footing, the word "corporation" evokes a similar reaction as the name "Nixon" did thirty years earlier: contempt, revulsion, and distrust. Whereas Nixon attempted to defuse his image problem by taking a tragicomic

Kennedy-esque walk along a windswept beach—wearing black wingtips—the current public relations antidote to any image challenge is to embrace the "be nice and show you care" mantra wherever possible.

We're not opposed to corporate Nice-a-paloozas, but effective outreach must have a direct link to preventing or defusing attacks.

In the battle for public opinion, you can only spin a public that wants to be spun. If you are Bill Gates, one of the richest persons in the history of civilization, and the government is suing you for antitrust and trying to break up your company, it's absurd to think that appearing in TV advertisements wearing a Mister Rogers–style sweater will trick people into thinking you're a harmless, folksy guy. When the hounds arrive at your front door, your objective, after all, shouldn't be to get them to like you; it should be to get them to stop attacking you.

Huge companies, believe it or not, want to be loved. Capitalism has sparked monumental achievements, but all of its resources have never found a way to make people "feel good" about big business. Nevertheless, persuading people to see corporate juggernauts as cuddly koala bears shouldn't be the goal. Rather than going through the futile exercise of trying to get people to like your company, it is more feasible to get them to stop attacking your company.

A GIANT CAUGHT FLAT-FOOTED

Microsoft's struggle to remain whole is a seminal case in point. In 1997, the Justice Department and 20 states sued Microsoft on the grounds that it maintained a monopoly over operating systems and Web browsers. The main question was whether Microsoft should be allowed to bundle its Internet Explorer with its ubiquitous Windows operating system, thereby maintaining a competitive advantage over alternatives to Explorer.

The Justice Department and attorneys general involved said this so-called monopoly gave Microsoft a predetermined victory in the browser wars since every Windows user automatically had an Internet Explorer, which discouraged consumers from purchasing or downloading an alternative browser. Microsoft argued that Windows and Internet Explorer were linked together and came as a package.

By most accounts the sponsor of Microsoft's troubles was its main competitor, Netscape, whose chief executive, James Barksdale, was savvy in the ways of Washington.

Just because a company like Microsoft is brilliant at making software, it doesn't mean that it's good at everything. In fact, the more brilliant some people are in one area, the more oblivious they might be in another. Perhaps mindful of Gates's publicly stated disdain for Washington, Barksdale targeted his adversary's weakness in 1996 and had his attorney send an eight-page letter to the Justice Department accusing Microsoft of antitrust activity.

It wasn't that Microsoft didn't take Netscape seriously; it was that it had never viewed Washington, D.C.—ostensibly a city of pencil pushers and glad-handers, not innovators—as a competitive arena like Silicon Valley. And Washington, where Gates was weakest, was precisely where he was ambushed.

Up until the time of the antitrust suit, Microsoft's Washington representation consisted of a lone individual who operated out of a company sales office in nearby Chevy Chase, Maryland.

By most accounts, the company, still functioning as an entrepreneurial software enterprise, had to cobble together a legal, government relations, and advocacy campaign on the fly. Nor is there evidence that the different branches within the company were coordinating in Machiavellian lockstep with one another toward a common goal. Rather, hostilities against Microsoft were breaking out on a variety of fronts. The first of three brutal hearings was held in the fall of 1997, led by Utah senator Orrin Hatch, who was investigating Microsoft's market domination tactics. Then there was the conference sponsored by consumer advocate Ralph Nader, who accused Microsoft of unfairly dominating the Internet.

The company responded on three fronts: Its legal department was trying to prevent its breakup; the fledgling government relations unit was trying to play catch-up to establish a meaningful Washington office; and the public relations team was trying to soften Microsoft's rapacious reputation. One effort of Microsoft's team was to oppose an increase in the Justice Department's antitrust enforcement budget, which, no doubt, didn't sit well with government investigators.

Microsoft may not have known a lot about Washington, but the company did have resources. In addition to hiring top-flight attorneys, the company retained public relations firms, advertising agencies, and lobbyists to wage its battle for public opinion.

Why does public opinion matter in a case that is ostensibly going to be decided in a court of law? The answer is that the legal process cannot be separated entirely from the broader elements of persuasion. The Justice Department, with whom Microsoft would ultimately have to negotiate, is a political body made of individuals who read newspaper editorials and respond to congressional inquiries.

As the antitrust battle heated up, Microsoft launched numerous television advertisements, one of them featuring a blind child using a computer. The message of these "soft" communications: Microsoft is a force for good. More than 100,000 of Microsoft's most loyal retailers, customers, and shareholders joined a grassroots political network called "Freedom to Innovate." At the push of a laptop's "Send" button, this network would flood the capital with phone calls, letters, and e-mails.

Microsoft doubled its lobbying budget in 1998, hiring some of the nation's biggest names from both sides of the political aisle. The company activated lobbyists in the states that had filed suit. It also increased its funding to trade associations and funneled money to diverse think tanks, including the Brookings Institution, the Heritage Foundation, the Cato Institute, and the Progressive Policy Institute. The central message of the think tanks: Microsoft innovates, and innovation is essential to American economic leadership. The subtext, of course, was *Do you want to be responsible for crippling the U.S. economy?*

During the 1999–2000 election cycle, Microsoft contributed almost $5 million to federal candidates and political parties— almost three times what it had given during the previous three election cycles combined.

Anecdotal evidence suggests that the investment in government relations advocacy paid off. In 1997, presumably at the urging of Netscape, Senator Conrad Burns (R-MT) sent a letter to the Federal Trade Commission referencing having received "very troubling" information that Microsoft was engaged in anticompetitive behavior. At some point after the arrival of this letter, Microsoft contributed $184,000 to the Burns Telecommunications Center. Wrote the *Washington Post,* "Since the donation, Burns has been virtually mum on the antitrust issue, though the senator says Microsoft's generosity is not the reason."

In April 2000, Judge Thomas Penfield Jackson ruled that Microsoft had committed monopolization and attempted monopolization. The judge suggested breaking up the company into two units. The tsunami of legal, advocacy, and communications efforts continued, and in September 2001, the Justice Department announced that it would not seek to break up the company after all.

The case was settled in November 2001, Microsoft agreeing to share its application programming with third-party companies. But the company was to remain intact.

A LESSER PUNISHMENT

In crisis management and public affairs, one can rarely make a quantifiable correlation between the tactics employed and the impact of those tactics on the outcome of events. Did President Reagan's fear-inducing advertisements featuring a bear in the woods (symbolizing the Soviet Union) get him reelected by a landslide in 1984, or would he have been reelected by a landslide anyway? We'll never know for sure, of course; however, professionals can draw conclusions about probable cause-and-effect based on life experience and intuition.

Ultimately, Microsoft's antitrust battle was won in a court of law, but its advocacy and public relations efforts almost certainly impacted how influential audiences—perhaps even the Justice Department—perceived the company.

Was it the political contributions or was it Gates's TV appearances in folksy sweaters that did the trick? Our view is that Microsoft's willingness to expend vast resources on first-rate advocacy talent and tactics may not have persuaded anyone to *like* the company in the conventional sense of popularity, but it did have the aggregate effect of creating the mantle of an institution that American leaders didn't want to see ruined.

Americans have dual feelings about extreme success and power: We distrust success and power, and we want them checked. Nevertheless, Americans recognize, at another level, that these things are the bedrock of a thriving society. The very same America that wanted Microsoft checked didn't want the company wrecked. According to the *Washington Post*:

> Microsoft had a simple story to tell lawmakers in Capitol Hill: It would be unfair to penalize a company for success that helped set off the country's economic boom. They carry a poll by the firm of Democrat Peter Hart and Republican Robert Teeter showing that two-thirds of Americans believe that Microsoft benefits consumers and that the suit is wrongheaded.

The net net: *Microsoft may be a tough S.O.B., but they're our tough S.O.B.—a company that helped return the United States to the forefront of global commerce following an era when it had become fashionable to speculate about America's economic decline.*

There were, of course, second-guessers. Some pundits

predictably speculated that had Bill Gates been more philanthropic throughout his career, the Justice Department might not have sought to break up his company. Not so. Even had Gates been more philanthropic in the 1990s, it wouldn't have neutralized Netscape's (and others) serious competitive grievance with Microsoft. Second, it's entirely possible to be generous and still be attacked by detractors who don't believe they have benefited from your generosity. Gates, for example, had contributed $1 billion to the United Negro College Fund in 1999, but this didn't stop minority employees from suing Microsoft for discrimination in the workplace in 2001.

Microsoft's massive advocacy effort did not spare them the wrath of the Justice Department and 20 state attorneys general, but, in the end, the company was not broken up, and its ultimate penalties were probably "less bad" than they would have been had the company not fought back in the manner that it did.

Today, as of this writing, Bill Gates remains the richest man in the world. Microsoft, while facing marketplace challenges from the likes of Google, is still the world's largest software company, with annual revenues of $40 billion, up from $11.9 billion when the antitrust case began. Gates, having transitioned from brash upstart to industry elder statesman, was named one of *Time* magazine's Persons of the Year in 2005, but it had more to do with his staggering track record of philanthropy than the fact that he wore sweaters. With an endowment of $30 billion, the Gates Foundation is the largest in the world. In retrospect, the price Gates paid to fight the antitrust battle seems paltry when compared to what was preserved and how history will likely treat him.

CHAPTER 10

Dissuasion

It's not like Charlton Heston coming down from the mountain with two stone tablets.

—JEFFREY IMMELT, ON EXPECTATIONS SURROUNDING HIS
APPOINTMENT AS GENERAL ELECTRIC CEO

The objective of crisis management is often to make bad situations less bad. If conventional public relations has been disparaged as telling pretty lies, then crisis management should be praised as telling ugly truths.

Crisis management, by nature, is unpleasant work. Some news is intrinsically bad. There are no corporate executives giving each other high-fives in the hallway every time a media "hit piece" is averted. In crisis management, your reward is relief. There are no crisis management academies out there doling out statuettes for bad news averted. Nor are bonuses given out every time a disaster *doesn't* happen.

The art of making things *not* happen is called "dissuasion," which, in practical terms, means convincing attackers not to attack by introducing risk. Dissuasion focuses on defusing threats at their origin, and can include tactics as soft as public education or as aggressive as litigation. When Clinton supporters engaged in a scorched-earth investigation of leading Republicans' sex lives, this dissuasive technique almost certainly ensured the president's survival.

At the softer end of the dissuasion spectrum is inoculating important audiences against bad news. Inoculation, by definition, means to inject just enough of the virus or "bad news" into the system for the body to learn to accommodate it.

If bad news is coming no matter what, it shouldn't be given anywhere to hide. Rather, important audiences must be desensitized to it so that its onset is not a trauma. Sometimes bad news isn't specific; rather, it's climate-driven, like bull and bear stock markets. It's safe to assume, for example, that a period of unquestioned media affection will be followed by a period of vilification. There is no science to precisely handicap this, but there is life experience.

SOFT DISSUASION: INOCULATION FOR A "BIG SHOES TO FILL" PROBLEM

Few companies have a richer history than General Electric.

Throughout the 1990s, General Electric grappled with the mixed blessing of revered leadership. The best thing about having the legendary Jack Welch as CEO was the goodwill and aura of competence that Welch's name conveyed to GE's important audiences. The potential pitfall was that Welch's retirement was on the horizon. Welch had taken the company from $27 billion in sales in 1981 when he took the top job to $130 billion in 2000 when it came time to name a successor. The company's market value during Welch's reign skyrocketed from $13 billion to $500 billion—making GE the first company in recorded history to hit that mark. The business media, having grown accustomed to the "Hail, Welch!" narrative of the past twenty years, were ripe for a new—and probably snarky—headline.

No one was more aware of this intangible vicissitude than GE.

In crisis management and media circles in 2000, there was a fatalistic sense that whoever followed Welch would be doomed by virtue of, well, following Welch. The business press, which covers the news in narrative waves—consider how the boy wonder CEOs of the 1990s were morphed into accused master thieves of the 2000s—would likely be predisposed to positioning Welch's successor as a disappointment.

There was recent precedent for this kind of coverage. A handful of new CEOs, such as Coca-Cola's Roberto Goizueta and Xerox's Paul Allaire, were widely positioned as having failed in comparison to their legendary predecessors. In addition, there were other succession disappointments at blue-chip companies, including Lucent, Campbell Soup, British Airways, and Gillette.

None of this was lost on image-conscious GE, which had begun planning for Welch's retirement in 1994, more than six years before his successor was to be named. GE pursued a strategy of inoculating its key audiences through dissuasion, essentially establishing the specific narrative it *did not* want the business media to pursue—namely, the notion that Immelt wouldn't be up to the job.

One of the more amusing misconceptions about large corporations is that they have master plans for sensitive contingencies. The truth: No "they" don't. Not all the time, anyway. The approach to crisis management in many companies is to hope like hell the Feared Scenario doesn't hit.

Not so at GE. Rather than running from the looming succession machinations, GE embraced them, wrestled with them, as opposed to shucking and jiving its way through the process. Aptly, upon Jeffrey Immelt's appointment in November 2000 as Welch's successor, a *Wall Street Journal* editorial opined on some of the reasons why the new boss would prosper, including "GE is good at succession."

GE MANAGEMENT TRANSITION PHASE I: SILENCE DURING THE SELECTION PROCESS

Succession at GE had been a main business priority practically since GE's inception. In its 130-year history, GE has had only nine chief executives. Welch's predecessor, Reg Jones, took as many years to identify Welch as it took Welch to select Immelt.

Succeeding Welch, however, would be especially tricky because Welch had become a cultural icon in the media age, beyond the scale of anything the company had ever experienced.

GE divided its communications surrounding succession into two distinct phases, the operations/selections process itself, and post-announcement strategy.

The company's greatest advantage during the selection process was that Jack Welch's leadership was unquestioned. GE's board gave him the latitude and authority to manage the transition. One of the greatest challenges in succession is the factionalism of choosing a new boss. A campaign of sorts can ensue, which often consists of posturing and press leaks, and candidates sometimes test how hard they can push their public relations efforts. But GE was disciplined enough to remain in blackout mode about the succession. While there was plenty of gossip, it was clear from the outset that no one would be named CEO by courting the press or other external audiences.

Welch actively involved his board of directors in cultivating and selecting the new CEO. This gave the board a personal, not just fiduciary, investment in Welch's successor—and strong disincentive to traffic in the kind of gossip that could have aggravated the selection process. When *Fortune* magazine in the spring of 2000 inquired of Welch how the succession was going, Welch "wouldn't even say 'No comment'; he just sat in silence."

Such was the secrecy that Welch flew to also-rans' offices in different cities unannounced to let them know they didn't get the job. When it came time for Immelt to get the news, he was flown on a non-GE-chartered airplane, using a pseudonym, to Welch's Palm Beach home. By quarantining news about the specifics of the selection process, GE deprived a potentially hostile media of a target ripe for division and exploitation. Simply put, a unified—and silent—GE gave the media nothing to divide and exploit.

GE MANAGEMENT TRANSITION PHASE II: TARGETED COMMUNICATIONS

Once Immelt was named to succeed Welch, the news embargo was lifted. It was time for Immelt to meet the press. If the introduction of risk is key to dissuasion, that risk came primarily in the form of a CEO-elect willing to talk candidly about the challenges that lay ahead for him.

Immelt had two overriding messages: (1) "I'm not Jack,"

and (2) "Don't expect a whirlwind of change." Immelt made it clear he would not compete with Welch, nor did he see himself as replacing him. Immelt deftly balanced being his own man— Immelt has a gentle giant's easygoing nature, whereas Welch is wiry and intense—with resisting the temptation to be too visionary too soon. His rhetoric was measured: "We've got incredible opportunities in our core businesses."

Had Immelt gone too far in the other direction, prematurely laying out "bold new visions," he could have been attacked on two fronts. First, the media would have been provoked to publicly ask, "Who does this upstart think he is, replacing Welch?" Rather, the media accepted Immelt's frank but deferential tone, characterized by one *Business Week* cover story titled "The Education of Jeff Immelt."

Second, a theoretically cocky Immelt may have aggravated GE stalwarts, including Welch, who may have seen a "bold new vision" approach as a slap in the face, providing the media with a menagerie of disgruntled inside sources.

During the transition, some questioned whether Welch would let Immelt have the stage. Welch, in the ultimate dissuasive act, deprived the business press of any opportunity to imply a clash of egos. To his credit, he stated publicly that Immelt's career results had been as impressive as Welch's own.

Immelt underscored that he was already taking over a GE that was well run, noting in a *Business Week* article after his appointment, "The way the company is run is the way I'm most comfortable with." (In fact, one of the merits of the selection process was that all of the finalists had been actively running huge divisions of the company for years.)

GE's outreach was characterized by a lack of "spin" in the conventional sense of hard-selling a vivid narrative. Rather than running from the perils of succession, Immelt appeared to embrace them.

During the time between Immelt's appointment and his early days as CEO, Immelt met with the world's leading business journalists, emphasizing the two publications that would be most likely to examine transition dynamics, *Fortune* and *Business Week*. *Fortune*'s January 8, 2001, article asked the question of Immelt in its subhead, "Does he have the best job in the world? Or the worst?" In the article's text, Immelt observed, "The outside world is saying, 'We're not sure you can do it.' The inside world is saying, 'Just watch us.'" He added, "I think longevity is a function of two things. It's a function of performance and your own ability to reinvent yourself. I think there will be zero honeymoon for me, so performance will have to be a given."

Immelt could not have been more right. Immelt took over GE on September 10, 2001, one day before the biggest hostile act on American soil. Soon after, Enron collapsed, and Immelt was forced to answer hard questions about his company's accounting practices, something Welch never had to do. "There will be zero honeymoon," Immelt had wisely said, "[but longevity] is a function of performance."

Immelt was able to strike the right balance with the rhetoric of vulnerability. In an earlier *Fortune* story, which was published shortly before 9/11, Immelt candidly discussed darker days in his career when Welch threatened to fire him for poor performance while he was running the plastics division. Welch also cited this example in his new book. The benefit? Like a forest ranger that lights a fire in order to control it, GE was depriving a potentially hostile media of the opportunity to go digging for skeletons.

While no one could have seen 9/11 and Enron's collapse coming, GE's visceral sense that *something* would provoke negative coverage early in Immelt's tenure was as vague as it was prescient. The company took a long-term view, understanding that if history was to be any guide, Immelt could be running GE for twenty years. Accordingly, management recognized the hazards of blustering in a climate where the media didn't want to be blustered.

Sometimes people will forgive a leader for not being the Messiah if he can convince them that he can take a beating. Doing so doesn't always require silky smoothness either. In a *Business Week* story that ran six months into Immelt's tenure, the new CEO was quoted as having responded angrily to a critical media report about the company's accounting practices: "It would be different if the stock price went down because we didn't meet expectations. Shit. I hate it when the stock goes down. The stock is my job. But we're doing what we said we'd do."

A slip of the tongue? Hardly. In an era when corporate America is being pilloried for being dishonest, a company boss who is able to convey candor—even with an expression of anger—is a good thing. The only thing more offensive than a dishonest CEO is a weak one. When you're under fire, there is no correlation between how sweet you are with how well you will be treated by the news media. It was essential for Immelt to establish early in his tenure one of the tenets of dissuasion: Do not be so needy of short-term praise that you are willing to permit inaccurate media coverage.

While some may have bristled at his candor, Immelt was rewarded at the very least by the GE family. An intracompany survey showed 80 percent of employees approving of his leadership. Wrote *Business Week,* "They love his enthusiasm, his vision, and his common-guy touch."

The ultimate factor that may have accrued to Immelt's benefit was not something he did, but something Jack Welch failed to do: close the Honeywell deal. The proposed Honeywell merger, which was to be the largest ever between two industrial giants, met its demise in the summer of 2001, when European Union leaders concluded it would stifle competition. Wrote *Time,* "Never before have officials outside the U.S. nixed a merger between two giant American corporations already approved by the DOJ." By the time Immelt assumed leadership, America had been diminished by 9/11 and Jack Welch, who had postponed his retirement to supervise the merger, had been diminished by the European Union. His enormous shoes that Immelt was expected to fill were reduced a size or two.

Regrettably, dissuasion is often a very aggressive game, one designed to put attackers on the defensive in order to defuse hostility, rather than get good news out. GE's dissuasion was anticipatory and high-minded. While the company didn't hesitate to throw a little attitude in its critics' direction, it wasn't a hardball strategy.

In 1998, Bill Clinton loyalists dissuaded Congress from removing him from office by conducting a scorched-earth exposé of his Republican critics. In 2004, President Bush's supporters dissuaded what they believed to be a biased media from further attacking his Vietnam-era record by demonstrating that a CBS *60 Minutes II* report was compiled using forged documents provided by Bush's enemies. In 1992, General Motors dissuaded potential litigants and the news media from further attacks on its products by exposing how *Dateline NBC* rigged the explosion of its pickup trucks in an effort to demonstrate their flammability. In 2002, Ringling Brothers and Barnum·& Bailey Circus dissuaded animal rights activists from further attacking it by proving in court that the animal abuse allegation leveled by the Humane Society was unfounded.

These dissuasive efforts required a combination of attitude, political-style mobilization, and good, old-fashioned detective work. Perhaps the most important factor in dissuasion is rejecting the premise that any attack on a successful business or institution is somehow noble and just. The hypersensitive, self-flagellating culture, which increasingly predominates in the post-Enron/WorldCom boardroom, sees many dissuasive campaigns as being somehow immoral. Gentility, compromise, and expressions of contrition are the coin of the post–boardroom scandal realm. Pliant postures are appropriate when one has wronged, but they deliver no respect when one is on the right side of an issue. If you're guilty, repent; if you're innocent, dissuade.

HARD DISSUASION

Whereas GE had an aura of omnipotence going into its management transition process, most individuals and companies in their struggles with potential adversaries do not. In GE's case the business media recognized that they would be dealing with Immelt potentially for decades and that incurring his wrath, while within their rights, might be unwise.

Not long ago, a client of ours—we'll call them the Central Appliance Company to protect their privacy—was facing an investigative report from a television news magazine program we'll call *Confidential Exposé*. The program was set to allege that Central Appliance's Blendex blender had been cutting off the fingers of consumers who used the product.

After discussing the potential hazards of Blendex, the company remained adamant that, if properly used, Blendex did not hurt consumers. But Confidential Exposé told the company that its report, which was scheduled to air in a week, would feature consumers who had been injured. The program had offered Central Appliance a chance to be interviewed on-camera, but we felt it was going to be a "hit piece," and saw little incentive to cooperate. We braced our client for the worst, including decent, honest consumers who would display their severed fingers before rolling cameras.

The first dissuasive tactic we employed was sending a letter from Central Appliance's attorneys to the general counsel of the Global News Network (again, a fictitious name), the broadcaster of *Confidential Exposé*. In the letter to Global, we questioned the show's intended claims and wanted another two weeks to verify them. We put the network on notice that Global News appeared to be treading on a line of argument that could be false and defamatory to the manufacturers of the Blendex blender, and that the company would defend its product even if it meant initiating libel litigation.

Predictably, Global News accused Central Appliance of

using bully tactics and attempting to stifle free speech, and declined to delay its report for a week. Central Appliance's general counsel explained to Global News that she wasn't questioning their right to free speech, just the network's right to defame her company. This subtle but important nuance is forever a point of contention between journalists, who rightly want to protect free speech, and corporations (and individuals) who rightly don't want to be defamed by false information. The network did agree to share with us the names of the plaintiffs' attorneys who had supplied *Confidential Exposé* with its on-air victims. Once we knew who the attorneys were, it was easy to track the purported victims, which would be the key to our dissuasive strategy.

Central Appliance's public relations director had been opposed to bringing in attorneys, considering it heavy-handed. He had simply wanted the opportunity to brief *Confidential Exposé*'s staff on Blendex's safety. "Where's the risk to [pressure on] the TV network?" our firm countered. We supported the idea of presenting a product safety demonstration to the network's staff, but they would have seen the request as PR puffery without some sort of threat. The presentation was held back for the time being.

While our client was disappointed that the network wasn't going to give us more time, we weren't surprised: Networks rarely cancel or delay stories based upon one legal letter. Nevertheless, the message had been sent: *Confidential Exposé*'s report was going to be intensely scrutinized and, if its reporters were reckless and defamed Blendex, there would be consequences.

We cross-referenced our safety reports with the names of *Confidential Exposé*'s proposed on-camera victims. We determined most of the wounds would have been highly unlikely if the blender had been operated properly. Moreover, the attorney representing the on-camera victim had a track record of being fined for launching frivolous litigation. Global News was informed of all of this in a subsequent letter from Central Appliance's general counsel, who offered a company spokesperson on the condition that the network allow a background briefing on Blendex's safety. This presentation, our attorney argued, would demonstrate the unlikelihood that Blendex could cause the kind of damage we knew that *Confidential Exposé* planned to suggest.

The network then agreed to sit for the presentation in which our case for Blendex's safety was laid out in forensic detail.

After the successful presentation, the plaintiffs' lawyer argued that his clients were being smeared by Central Appliance's investigation. Global News, however, was sufficiently swayed that the victims' stories were not credible. They declined to feature them in *Confidential Exposé*'s planned report. The plaintiff's lawyer was angry, of course, because he was depending upon this report to influence a potential jury that might be watching the program and might sympathize with the plaintiffs.

The result: *Confidential Exposé* aired a brief version of a report alleging a potential hazard with Blendex. None of the "walking wounded" footage we feared aired because our presentation had impeached the credibility of the would-be victims. The final segment included a Central Appliance spokesperson demonstrating how the blender could be secured properly in order to avoid a hazard. While the story didn't vanish, its hard edge was significantly softened, and Central Appliance actually benefited from what was essentially a public service announcement on how to use the product safely.

This comparatively happy ending did not occur because

Global News experienced an epiphany due to enlightenment or an empty-handed appeal to fairness. Rather, Central Appliance was willing to go nose-to-nose with a powerful media network and introduce risk in the form of litigation, potential damages, and embarrassment if they had run with the hit piece that had been initially planned. It was the combination of our client's will to fight and the pedigree of its evidence that dissuaded the network from attacking a good product made by a good company.

CHAPTER 11

Do the Media's Job for Them

Where would I get a damned finger, for God's sake?

—ANNA AYALA, WENDY'S SEVERED-FINGER FRAUDSTER

I t was one of the strangest inquiries we've ever received. A young reporter for an antibusiness online publication called our firm and, with a snort, asked what our role had been in the "smearing" of activist Rachel Carson upon the publication of her seminal environmental book, *Silent Spring*. We asked the reporter if she knew what year the book had been published. She huffed that she didn't know in a manner to suggest we were spinning her with a technicality. We finally informed her that most of us had yet to be born by the year of *Silent Spring*'s publication and could not have had any role in a smear campaign. After a beat, she responded, "They told me you were good."

We like to think we're good at crisis management, too, but we certainly hadn't exhibited much talent for it prior to our births. Yet this reporter, hell-bent on doing a hit piece on us, presumably because of our work for industrial interests, would only be dissuaded by one thing: It was a physical impossibility for us to have been involved in whatever skullduggery she was alleging *because we hadn't been born yet!*

It is widely assumed by those who find themselves under attack that the media have some kind of scientific litmus test for determining whether a story is fit to be printed or aired. And respectable media institutions *do* have their standards, but there is something insidious—and very human—at work in the preparation of a hit piece: the media's desire to believe in the evil of their targets.

Journalists on the attack are human beings who can be vested in an unwavering conviction that their targets are uniquely worthy of injury or exposure. Never mind protestations of I'm-just-looking-for-the-truth objectivity; a hit piece is a hunting expedition, and the only good target is a bloody target. This phenomenon was very likely at work in the 2004 *60 Minutes II* report on President Bush's Vietnam-era war record, where the probable combination of political bias, time pressure, and a pre-set conviction that Bush had ducked combat led a seasoned journalist like Dan Rather to gloss over fraudulent documents that would have been more carefully vetted under different circumstances.

Bush loyalists, trusting neither CBS's version nor its motives, got to work on the blogosphere. Bloggers did the job *60 Minutes II* should have done in the first place, demonstrating that the documents implicating Bush were, in fact, forgeries. Venerable CBS was embarrassed, a top-flight producer was deposed, and Dan Rather apologized shortly before leaving *60 Minutes II* and retiring from his network anchor's position.

The impossibility of objectivity, combined with increased competition, dwindling news budgets, and declining journalism standards, has shifted the burden of proof from the media to the target. Whereas the old school of public relations required the education of hostile media, modern crisis management rejects the notion that a hostile journalist is open to being educated. The objective, therefore, becomes either to dissuade the media from running with a hostile story by introducing risk to the news outlet, or constructing a better story oneself.

FINGER FOOD: AN ALTERNATIVE NARRATIVE IN THE WENDY'S CHILI INCIDENT

In March 2005, news flashed across the country that thirty-nine-year-old Anna Ayala had found a severed human finger in a container of Wendy's chili in San Jose, California. It was a disgusting revelation, and the sheer visual, emotional, and late-night comic power of this spectacle overwhelmed any alternative narrative that Wendy's had readily available when the crisis hit.

Executives at Wendy's, rightly proud of their long-standing reputation for serving quality foods in sanitary conditions, were skeptical of Ayala's claim, especially when she began making noises about suing the company. Wendy's, in concert with local health authorities and the police, inspected the hands of Wendy's employees and found no severed fingers. The company made the requisite assurances to the public that its food supply was safe, and offered a $50,000 reward to anyone who could provide information that would help trace the origin of the finger found in the chili. Business fell off sharply—as much as 50 percent—at Wendy's outlets in Northern California. Reported the *San Jose Mercury News*, "No one is suggesting it was a con, such as the old scams like putting a bug in food or a mouse in a soda bottle to get money."

Wendy's reputation was in limbo because something was missing besides a finger: a simple explanation for how a severed human finger had found its way into a cup of Wendy's chili. To make matters worse, the media insisted on accompanying many of its stories with a photograph of the severed finger, which reinforced a distressingly vivid storyline—a woman found a severed finger in her Wendy's chili, and you might too!

Both crisis creation and crisis management involve storytelling. It thus was in the media's self-interest to keep repeating the core allegation and top it off with a revolting visual. The consumer public couldn't get enough of the gross-out story of the year.

On the crisis management side of the equation, consumers wanted to know how the tale would end. In the case of food, drug, and health-related crises, consumers want simple answers to two questions: *Am I going to be okay?* and *What are you doing about it?*

In the absence of a clear answer, the best Wendy's could do was demonstrate the company's commitment to finding answers, which included dispatching a private investigations team to parallel the San Jose Police's investigation. Wendy's executives communicated constantly with the press but were candid about their frustration. Said Wendy's spokesman Denny Lynch,

"What you chase are the real facts, and that is the challenge. The corporation is put on the defensive the moment it happens."

In the meantime, Wendy's had to contend with the narrative locomotive, which came in the form of the constant visual display of the severed finger. In a shrewd stopgap maneuver to neutralize unpleasant optics, Wendy's agreed to conduct television interviews about the crisis on the condition that the TV station not show the ubiquitous photo of the severed finger.

In the month following Ayala's initial report, San Jose Police searched her home. The photo of a severed finger began to be replaced in the media with images of police raiding Ayala's residence. As the spotlight fell on Ayala, Wendy's doubled its award offer for information. With significant prompting from Wendy's and law enforcement, Ayala's past began to become a focus of coverage. Ayala bristled at the suggestion that the whole affair was an extortion scam, saying, "That is very sick, sick, sick. It's disgusting. You're playing with the human race."

The media began to report that Ayala had been involved with a half-dozen legal battles in the San Francisco area, including a lawsuit against an ex-supervisor for sexual harassment and a lawsuit against several automotive companies, claiming that a wheel had fallen off her car. It was also learned that Ayala's family had received a settlement for medical expenses after her daughter became ill after eating at a Las Vegas Mexican restaurant.

If there was one word that defined news coverage during the opening weeks of the crisis, it was "finger." As the weeks passed, however, a new word was inserted into the Wendy's crisis lexicon: grifter.

In mid-April, Ayala was arrested at her home for attempted

grand theft and for an unrelated charge of grand theft involving the sale of a mobile home. On May 13, police announced that the finger that had been "found" in Ayala's chili had come from a workplace associate of Ayala's husband who had severed it in a routine industrial accident. The associate had apparently owed Ayala's husband $50, but the husband took the finger in lieu of cash. Ayala and her husband pleaded guilty.

The revelation that Ayala was a criminal who had placed the finger in her chili accomplished several objectives. First, it demonstrated that the source of the problem was external to Wendy's—that the company was not responsible for the disturbing discovery. Second, action had been taken to ensure public safety.

The two bellwether questions of crisis management had been answered:

Q. Am I going to be okay?
A. Yes, because the allegation was fraudulent. Severed fingers don't turn up in Wendy's chili.
Q. What are you doing about it?
A. We're punishing the perpetrator, and thanking our consumers for believing in us in the form of coupons. . . .

According to Wendy's Lynch, sales at Northern California's Wendy's have rebounded, but not quite to precrisis levels. Wendy's managed its crisis through a combination of making human connections with its consumers, fostering the possibility that foul play was at work, playing dissuasive hardball with media insistent on trafficking in the severed finger photo, and cooperating with authorities to expose the provenance of the crime in order to bring the perpetrator to justice. Recognizing the story the media wanted to do, Wendy's (with external support) helped create an alternative narrative that did not seem to interest some media initially.

The Wendy's case wasn't the first time the do-the-media's-job model of crisis management had been employed to great effect. In 1993, rumors surfaced that syringes had been discovered in cans of Diet Pepsi. Like Wendy's, PepsiCo made assurances that tampering of this nature was all but impossible. In a classic instance of using media technology as the answer, the company encouraged film crews to record the soft drink manufacturing process, which included 1,200 cans per minute being cleaned, filled with soda, and sealed. Any reasonable person seeing this evidence would conclude that in-plant syringe tampering was highly improbable.

Still, reports of syringes continued to surface for a week until a Colorado supermarket security camera picked up a woman trying to insert a syringe into a soft drink can. This image shut down the crisis.

INVESTIGATIVE REPORTING AS A CRISIS MANAGEMENT FUNCTION

In any human controversy, people ask themselves an intuitive question: What happened here? Human beings will be in a state of distress until that question is answered. Modern crisis management puts the burden of vindication on the attack target. In both the Wendy's and Pepsi cases, the media had been committed to a certain narrative until the attack targets—with the help of the authorities—began to lay out a plausible alternative scenario.

Our firm routinely parallels the investigations into our clients that are launched by the media. We employ former investigative reporters who spent decades examining business and political targets for major print and broadcast media. These resources were brought to bear when a pharmaceutical client, which manufactured a psychoactive drug we'll call Placidon in this composite example, came under fire.

Placidon was such an effective mood stabilizer that people who didn't necessarily need the drug sought to obtain it. Leading media outlets began reporting that Placidon's manufacturer was aggressively distributing the drug ostensibly to "hook" more potential users. Judging from the news reports, Placidon wasn't a medical godsend as much as it was a street drug being trafficked by a blue-chip pharmaceutical company.

One member of our client's crisis team suggested that we attempt to educate the media about all of the patients who had benefited from Placidon. Skeptical, we tried this, but few journalists were interested. To the media, this was a crime story and Placidon's manufacturer was the criminal. This would not be an easy narrative to shift.

Under profound stress to stop the hemorrhage of brutal coverage, we suggested another approach: conducting our own investigation of precisely who was abusing Placidon.

"We're not investigative reporters," the client bristled.

"We are now," we replied.

During a several-month period, our firm initiated an investigation of Placidon's distribution. There was good news and bad news. The bad news was that the drug was genuinely being abused in plenty of cases. The good news, however perverse, was that those who were abusing the drugs were criminals. The news media, by and large, had been positioning Placidon's abusers as everyday people who had become hooked on a drug that was pushed on them by an avaricious pharmaceutical company. One person, who had been held out as a sympathetic poster child of Placidon abuse in a lengthy magazine profile, turned out to be a crooked cop who had been kicked off his police force several years earlier for drug trafficking. Another man, featured sympathetically in a news story, who had given a fatal overdose of Placidon to a woman, turned out to be a convicted rapist.

In the initial round of Placidon coverage, most journalists, for whatever reason, had no interest in deviating from their narrow story line: *Placidon is a bad drug and it's all the company's fault.* Once we were able to introduce two new variables—that the abusers were hardened criminals, not ordinary patients; and that the news media had ignored vital information that contradicted their narrative—we were then able to communicate the positive contribution Placidon had made to the lives of patients.

To accomplish this, we not only had to devote vast resources to conducting an investigation (with no guarantee of results), but our client had to be willing to embarrass the media that had been so critical of Placidon. Most companies understandably have a visceral discomfort with the notion of embarrassing journalists. There's a catch, however: The news media are not monolithic. One news outlet is willing to be critical of a rival outlet, provided that there is ample evidence of journalistic wrongdoing.

As much as it has become fashionable to bash the news media in recent years, there is something about seeing a story in print or on television that lends a mantle of judicial authority. The very same people who may roll their eyes at the media privately view news coverage as a sanctification of truth. People are understandably reluctant to disrespect this mantle. Nevertheless, when the might of the media is turned against an individual or institution, the effects can be ruinous. While it may not be wise under normal circumstances to challenge the media, crises and marketplace assaults are not normal circumstances. They are zero-sum struggles in which the winner will be the party who takes an audacious position supported by first-rate reporting, not necessarily the more venerable media institution.

CHAPTER 12

When the Judge and Jury Need to Know

> The prosecution was broadcasting on AM, but the jury was receiving on FM.
>
> —PUNDIT AFTER THE O. J. SIMPSON VERDICT

His life as he knew it was over. A legendary figure in the business world, this fallen Captain of Industry had spent the better part of two decades smiling sagaciously into a camera lens with his fists pressed against his desk. The emblematic message: This was a man with the Answer, the man everybody in business wanted to be. A magician of commerce.

Then he was cuffed by the FBI and frog-marched into court for making billions of dollars disappear from HugeCo's corporate coffers and retirement plans.

The Captain, of course, is a composite of clients and nonclients past, present, and future who finds himself embroiled in a legal battle that will define his life. He may just as easily be a celebrity defendant as a business icon. Regardless of what category he falls into, the proverbial Captain has certain attributes that can be found across cases.

First, he is innocent. He is the victim of overzealous prosecutors and envious former colleagues. There is nothing—nothing—to the charges against him. This is not an act either. He is not a Machiavellian genius who knows in his heart that he's an S.O.B. and is putting on an act in order to win his freedom. He is passionate about his innocence.

Second, he believes his innocence will prove self-evident. "Wait until you see what I've got on my accuser." His accuser is uniquely corrupt, and somewhere, in a file, there is evidence that will "blow you away."

Third, he cannot bear being hated. He wants to be understood. That's right, the Captain—the man who has become the butt of late-night comedy monologues as a living symbol of avarice—wants you to like him. He wants to tell you the story of what really happened at HugeCo.

Perhaps most frustrating for a crisis manager, the Captain may have been told by his lawyer and his public relations whiz that come hell or high water, his side of the story will "get out there," and they're just the ones to pull it off. In all likelihood, Lawyer No. 1 and PR Flack No. 1 won't last very long. As reality sets in, the Captain will panic and sense that he may have been lied to. Even if Lawyer No. 1 and PR Flack No. 1 have been honest from the start, the Captain, terrified to his marrow, will become angry that this initial team has not been able to stop the onslaught.

When we first meet with the Captain, usually a few months into his ordeal, he tells us he's read some of our publications and thinks we're the right ones for the job. We explain that while we've got a strong track record, we're not saviors. The Captain claims to understand this, but he doesn't; in his defense, he can't: He needs us to be saviors.

The thing he really wants, he tells us at great length, is to get his "message out." That's when Lawyer No. 2 and we tell him the governing principle of our work together: We want him to be acquitted. Period.

The Captain has been cast in a very specific narrative. He is the villain in this story. In the storytellers' script, he is the reason why billions of dollars vanished from HugeCo. While the Captain insists that the situation is "more complex than that" (and he's right), we explain to him that within days, the public will see irrefutable proof of his guilt. This stuns him. "What do you know that I don't?" he asks. "After all, you've only been on my case for a few hours."

What we understand that the Captain doesn't is how proof of guilt is conveyed in the Information Age. In addition to the facts of the case, it will be conveyed in narrative form using archetypal images. A montage in the print and electronic media will appear that will contain the following images: (1) The Captain's "perp walk" into court; (2) an aerial view of the Captain's mansion; (3) a timeline of his assets and acquisitions and possessions, which may or may not include a photo of his alluring (and younger) second wife; and (4) a juxtaposed photograph of an honest soul in his sixties who lost his retirement funds in the Captain's company.

Lawyer No. 2 will interject at this point that our version of proof is different from a judge's version. This is true. In court, a judge probably won't allow the aerial view of the Captain's house to be admitted as evidence. Still, both the Captain and Lawyer

No. 2 get my point: An aerial view may not be evidence in the forensic sense, but it matters.

The only way to combat the devastating narrative that the prosecution and the news media have in store for us is to create an alternative narrative of the Captain's exploits. This alternative narrative, however, will not be crafted to win hearts and minds in the broader sense. Rather, it will be crafted for a judge and jury who will decide the Captain's fate. In this version, the Captain may not be deemed lovable, but he may be deemed not guilty.

Lawyer No. 2 is a storyteller. So are we. The difference between us is that Lawyer No. 2 must tell the story that the law strictly allows. As communicators, we operate in murky terrain between the law and emotion. On one hand, we must respect the law, but on the other, we may encourage the Captain to tap into sentiments that are extralegal. These sentiments must, of course, support the legal case, but they won't necessarily be legal arguments.

We want the potential jury pool to know that the Captain never dumped his company's stock on the sly. The prosecutor wants people to believe that the Captain cashed out when he had inside information that his company was tanking. We want the judge to be concerned about the prosecutor's media grandstanding that will render it almost impossible for the Captain to get a fair trial in a city deeply resentful of his company's collapse. Perhaps this will support Lawyer No. 2's efforts to get a change of venue. We want the jury to remember that the witnesses against the Captain have been given tremendous incentive to blame the Captain, not themselves, for HugeCo's collapse. If we get it right, the jury won't trust the Captain's accusers.

We want the jury to be mindful of the Captain's civic works, that he was a giver to the community, not a taker from it. We want them to ask what motive could the Captain have had to harm HugeCo. We want the jury to distinguish between a company that failed and criminal behavior. It is possible, after all, for companies to fail because of marketplace conditions and not criminality.

The hardest question we've ever been asked by a client about litigation communications and crisis management is: "Does it work?"

The most honest answer is: "Sometimes." Put differently, we don't know if engaging communications specialists will always help when you're going to court, but we do know that it's not smart to be without this kind of support.

In the current frenzy of anticorporate witch hunts, academics, journalists, and consultants are rushing to declare that high-stakes communications efforts have been mishandled by inept attorneys and public relations people. A case lost is a case botched, or so the logic goes. If Martha Stewart had only pleaded or apologized or performed a triple axel while hugging a homeless person of the right demographic, "it" all would have gone away.

While most of these chestnuts of hindsight diagnosis should be dismissed as the musings of a Greek chorus that has never actually played a part in one of these dramas, there is one line of debate that merits examination: the natural tension between attorneys and public relations people.

As a rule, attorneys want their besieged client—be it a manufacturer accused of making a faulty product or engaging in an unethical marketing practice, or a CEO under indictment—to be silent. Too much chatter, of course, is risky and can create trouble in court. Martha Stewart is a primary case in point; it was Stewart's comments *after* being accused of insider trading that got her into trouble.

The very same silence, however, that is legally shrewd can be problematic business-wise. In the Age of Corporate Malfeasance, it is not guilt that convicts a business or individual, it's often suspense—the mystery, the not-knowing. Shareholders, consumers, employees, and regulators demand to know the fundamentals of the matter: What happened here? Are we going to be safe? Will the company survive? What's being done about it? Taking the proverbial Fifth and blaming one's attorneys for silence may work in court but not in the marketplace.

Unfortunately, there are no hard and fast rules for litigation communications and crisis management, but there are lessons to be learned from many years of racking up wins, losses, and compromises. What follows are the unvarnished "facts of life"— including practical words of counsel—about engaging in legal communications.

THE JUDGE AND JURY ARE YOUR TARGETS

Staying out of jail is more important than looking good. Just ask O. J. Simpson. He may be despised, but he's free and playing golf. A similar lesson applies to business litigation: It's more important to win the case than it is to have everybody love you.

In the O. J. Simpson case, a pundit wisely remarked that the prosecution was communicating on "AM" while the jury was "receiving on FM." While the prosecution was talking about the facts of the case, the jury was "receiving" personally relevant experiences with racism. Simpson's defense met the jury's demands, which is why they prevailed.

While judges and jurors aren't supposed to glean information from the news media, they do. This is one reason why prosecutors demand "perp walks." They want a potential jury to get the message: *This person is a criminal.* In the Captain's case, the prosecution will attempt to position him as a typical big-business villain. In the city where his trial will be held, however, the Captain's humble, local roots may be important to the jury. We believe there's a good chance that the jury will be distrustful of the federal government's efforts to lay a web of complicated transactions at the feet of a local boy made good.

In some of the corporate scandal cases we have worked on, the hope of broad cultural vindication must be set aside in favor of identifying arguments and juror personality types that may lead to acquittal. Is it really important that everyone love your client? Sure, it would be nice, but is it doable? Probably not. Acquittal in court, on the other hand, may be possible, and, in the short term at least, should be the primary goal.

There is a divergence, however, in what the Captain wants and what his defense team wants. Whereas the Captain wants to save face in the eyes of the community, Lawyer No. 2 and I are focused solely on his acquittal. The subtle difference is that the Captain wants more noise made about his charity and his awe-inspiring leadership. His defense team, however, believes this approach may provoke incredulity, if not nausea. We want the jury to believe it's possible that the Captain was a less-than-perfect leader who might, in fact, have been conned by underlings. If the jury believes the Captain is Superman, then it stands to reason that he should have known what was going on at his company. In the end, the strategy will be the Captain's choice, but his defense team will try to persuade him that it is in his best interests to influence the opinions of the community at large in order to persuade the jury, not vice versa.

WE ARE IN A UNIQUELY HOSTILE CLIMATE

The advice one gives a client cannot be separated from the climate in which it occurs. The current anticorporate atmosphere, due to a combination of scandals and dimming wealth horizons, is partly cyclical. A good lawyer and communicator can navigate in this climate, not change it. For the time being, the public, media, and government are motivated more by vengeance than justice—the desire to see powerful people injured as a result of tangible hardship. A loss in a court of law or public opinion doesn't necessarily mean a strategy failed.

IDENTIFY WHAT'S DOABLE, NOT WHAT'S IDEAL

Litigation support efforts can be doomed by utopian expectations. Of particular concern is the false expectation that audiences want to hear the message of an unsympathetic figure. In a climate characterized by virulent distrust of business, education doesn't defuse outrage. Making the Firestone brand popular after the media feeding about faulty tires on Ford Explorers was simply not doable. Settling the lawsuits and resurrecting the company under the Bridgestone brand was.

In Michael Jackson's child molestation trial, the very same jury that may have found the defendant to be peculiar found the mother of his accuser to be "walking, talking reasonable doubt," according to one trial watcher.

Janet Arviso was a schemer to her core, with a record of serial litigation, welfare fraud, and making sexually charged allegations against those with the means to pay her. It came to light during Jackson's trial that she had reached a $150,000 settlement with JC Penney for allegedly kidnapping and sexually abusing her. Arviso made these allegations after her son—the same son who was Michael Jackson's accuser—was discovered in possession of the department store's goods minus the receipts to prove he paid for them. The *London Times* reported:

> In the JC Penney case, Ms. Arviso had said under oath that her husband, David, had never hit her, and that her bruising had been caused by the store's security guards. Then, during her divorce, she claimed she was a battered wife. This was perhaps her biggest mistake. The singer's defense team was able to destroy her credibility from the moment its cross-examination began.

Celebrity witnesses such as Jay Leno voiced their assessments of Arviso as a grifter. And then, during her testimony, Arviso proceeded to excoriate the jury, who interpreted her finger-wagging outbursts as a sign that they had failed to recognize her importance. The jury found it plausible that a woman with a shakedown pedigree, who seemed so desperate to live the life of a tantrum-throwing Hollywood player, would leverage her child and make hideous allegations for money.

With corporate defendants, the objective is acquittal in court, not public adulation. With corporations under siege, the objective is getting back to business, not the hackneyed notion of "winning hearts and minds" about the beauty of free enterprise. Attorneys and clients alike embrace the utopian—and emotionally satisfying—promises of public relations people at their peril.

DIFFERENTIATE BETWEEN WHAT'S STRATEGIC AND WHAT'S THERAPEUTIC

Defendants and litigants tend to have difficulty differentiating between communications that are strategic and those that are therapeutic. People under fire want everybody to know everything. In trials and litigation, though, not everything matters. What matters is what the judge and jury thinks. To the extent that some of this information is derived from the media or other public opinion venues, that's fine, but "good PR" independent of courtroom utility isn't worth much.

DON'T ASSUME THE PUBLIC THINKS AS YOU DO

There are certain fundamental realities of public opinion that are hard to avoid. For one thing, the very same America that publicly claims to dislike trial lawyers is privately happy they're available to keep corporations in check. Furthermore, despite gripes from the business community about overzealous prosecutors—former New York attorney general Eliot Spitzer comes to mind—the public and the media believe these watchdogs are the good guys. Put differently, there is no risk whatsoever in this climate to anyone who would do a criminal defendant or corporation ill.

CHAPTER 13

Write Your Own Case History

Nothing succeeds like the appearance of success.

—CHRISTOPHER LASCH

Every crisis manager faces two challenges: managing the crisis and looking good in the process. Does the "looking good" part sound a bit superficial? It shouldn't. Conveying an impression of competent damage control isn't about pretense or ego. It is an absolutely crucial act of survival. Companies that act effectively behind closed doors but leave it to others to judge their efforts risk being portrayed as inept, arrogant, or worse. Sometimes simply "doing the right thing" is enough; at other times, gaining recognition for your crisis management labors must be a central part of your response.

Consider the event that has been labeled, perhaps unfairly, as one of the worst handled crises in corporate history—that of the *Exxon Valdez*. It all began just after midnight on March 24, 1989, when the tanker *Exxon Valdez* struck Bligh Reef in Prince William Sound, Alaska, releasing some 11 million gallons of crude oil. It was easily the largest oil spill in U.S. history, and, of course, the scale of environmental impact was overwhelming.

But routinely omitted from the retelling of this story is the fact that Alyeska, an association representing seven oil companies who operated in Valdez, in accordance with the area's contingency planning, first assumed responsibility for the cleanup. Moreover, according to the Environmental Protection Agency, the spill's "remote location—accessible only by helicopter and boat—made government and industry efforts difficult and tested existing plans for dealing with such an event." From the onset, bad weather delayed the arrival of vitally needed equipment and hampered cleanup efforts. Thick oil and heavy kelp clogged the equipment once it arrived. Repairs were time-consuming. The bad weather continued.

Ultimately, the Coast Guard and thousands of citizens and volunteers joined with Exxon to clean up as much of the mess as they could. The company spent $2.2 billion on the cleanup effort and voluntarily paid another $300 million to 11,000 Alaskans and businesses affected by the spill.

An Exxon employee made a horrible, unforgivable mistake. He was allegedly drunk at the helm. There's little question that stronger action should have been taken sooner. But this was not a case, as often portrayed, of an oblivious company ignoring its duties. In fact, a trial court commended the company for coming forward "with its people and its pocketbook and doing what had to be done under difficult circumstances." Three years later, the Coast Guard declared the cleanup complete and commended Exxon for its unprecedented effort.

But that story never got out. Instead, what got covered were heart-wrenching pictures of oil-coated birds and dying seals, juxtaposed against the failure of a company to swiftly put forth an executive who could express regret and outline the company's game plan. Reportedly, the company's CEO at the time—long known for his media wariness—waited six days to make a statement and did not visit the scene of the accident until three weeks after the spill. To be sure, statements and site visits like these are mostly symbolic, but sometimes symbolism is everything. Days later, the company took out full-page advertisements in newspapers nationally in an effort to get its story out, but the die had been cast.

Exxon has redoubled its efforts to more carefully control the shipment of oil, and today the company wins awards for its tanker-safety programs. But while the shores of Prince William Sound may have recovered, it took a lot longer for Exxon to restore its reputation. What the company had acquired was what we call a "character crisis," which is when the very moral fiber of the company—not just the events surrounding the crisis—comes into question. And once a company's or individual's character is in doubt—and the motivations behind its actions or inactions are reviled—it transforms into an "allegation magnet": Whatever it is accused of sticks, not necessarily because it is true but because it is the conduct we would expect from such a flawed personality. In short, we judge character as much as we judge behavior. If the accused character is in doubt, mob rule kicks in. The crisis endpoint quickly shifts from resolution of the problem to punishment of the accused.

RUDY GIULIANI: CRISIS MANAGER IN CHIEF

Let's consider the flip side of the coin. One master of the art of symbolic crisis management is the former mayor of New York City, the irrepressible Rudy Giuliani. Many people forget that prior to 9/11, Mr. Giuliani was teetering on the brink of public disdain and political irrelevancy. Indeed, on December 31, 2001, *Time* magazine's Eric Pooley, in a generally glowing profile of the mayor, described the state of his public image on the day prior to September 11 this way:

> . . . great swaths of the city were sick of him. People were tired of his Vesuvian temper and constant battles— against his political enemies, against some of his own appointees, against the media and city-funded museums, against black leaders and street vendors and jaywalkers and finally against his own wife. . . . New Yorkers seemed ready for Rudy and [future wife] Judi to leave the stage together and melt into the crowd.

But, as Pooley continued: "Fate had another idea. When the day of infamy came, Giuliani seized it as if he had been waiting all of his life. . . ." With the president safely circling the skies in Air Force One, Giuliani instantly emerged as the Crisis Manager in Chief. He seemed to be everywhere—calming the panicked, comforting the grieving, and flexing America's grit and determination in the face of a shocking and terrifying attack. Rudy Giuliani was the face of America during those first days, and the news media couldn't get enough of him.

It wasn't easy work. He hardly slept for days. One count had the mayor attending nearly two hundred funerals, services, and wakes for the firefighters, police officers, and emergency workers killed in the attack. Just as important, Giuliani understood the power of symbolic action in the face of a crisis. He relentlessly cajoled the city's most iconic institutions, such as the New York Stock Exchange and Yankee Stadium, to reopen as quickly as possible to demonstrate that New Yorkers were picking themselves up off the mat. If Wall Street is back, New York is back. If the Yankees are playing, a return to normalcy has begun.

Of course, as an elected official and seasoned politician, Mr. Giuliani understood from experience what the situation required. He also knew that reporters—especially political reporters—are a restless bunch. While they may start off covering the substance of a 9/11 crisis (Who were the attackers and how did it happen?), in short-order they will turn their attention to how its political leaders are responding to the challenge.

This understanding of how the news media can quickly turn highly critical on a business's crisis management performance is driving more and more companies to begin their communications efforts before calamity has even hit. By getting out early, companies can eliminate or minimize the perception that they are the party at fault. By demonstrating concern, preparedness, and preemptive action before a crisis hits, you can position yourself as part of the solution, as opposed to the problem. Preemption means no character crisis.

INOCULATING AGAINST HYSTERIA

In 2005, an outbreak of avian flu spread quickly through Asia, Europe, and Africa, and the impacts on the poultry industry were severe. Yum Brands, owners of Kentucky Fried Chicken, saw operating profit in fast-growing China plunge by 20 percent in one quarter alone. KFC estimates that U.S. sales could decline by an equal amount should the bird flu spread here. That would be a serious financial hit, to say the least. Moreover, the onslaught of media and consumer inquiry would be overwhelming. According to the Centers for Disease Control and Prevention, as much as 35 percent of the U.S. population could become sick from a pandemic flu. The wrongful association of bird flu with eating poultry products would be immediate, and perhaps devastating to a company like Kentucky Fried Chicken.

That is why it made eminent good sense for KFC to get out front—way out front—of the issue in November 2005 by announcing it had prepared an ad campaign to reassure consumers that its chicken was safe to eat in the event of a bird flu outbreak. The standby ads were leveraged to create free media opportunities, and a KFC spokesperson offered straightforward quotes such as: "The message is to reassure consumers that eating cooked chicken is perfectly safe. As our investors would hope, we are being proactive in preparing the materials in the event we need to use them." Suppliers Perdue Farms and Tyson Foods joined in by releasing similar press statements.

By communicating with a U.S. audience *before* a crisis occurred, chicken producers and processors got out their key messages about the safety of eating poultry, and they pre-positioned themselves as responsible companies armed to deal with potential consumer panic. In short, they were winning positive PR for their crisis management planning and readiness.

Of course, you can publicize your efforts to prepare for a crisis that never comes and look a little silly in the process. But no harm done. As 1999 closed, hundreds of companies—spurred by thousands of consultants—were wringing their hands about the apocalyptic threats of the coming Y2K computer meltdown. Remember? When the clock flipped to 2000, untold numbers of computers and high-tech systems—including commercial airliners in flight—were supposed to come crashing down. Myriad companies promoted their war rooms, call centers, preemptive debugging programs, and other efforts to avoid or respond to the pending doom. When the big day came, not a whole lot happened, but the idea was to be better safe than sorry. While there were a few gratuitous guffaws over all the unnecessary preparation, within a week the world had moved on and no one had egg on their face.

PERCEPTION IS REALITY

There are also many crises in which the fundamental challenge is to stem a loss of customers versus affecting public opinion. Especially for manufacturers, this means keeping downstream customers, applicators, and retailers from dropping their products like hot potatoes over safety or other allegations sparking public concern, consumer group criticism, or regulatory interest. Anyone who has been through this knows that the blunt message from customers, especially from retailers who are closest to the consumer, is "Don't make your problem my problem." They don't always want to be educated on the technical aspect of the problem, but they do need to be convinced you have an effective crisis management program to keep the heat off of them. It is all another element of doing PR for crisis management.

times the chief challenge with customers is to con-
that a few negative articles and a handful of calls or
e-mails into their call centers don't constitute a crisis of irrevers-
ible proportions. Winning this struggle over "perception versus
reality" can often be achieved by showing them hard data, such
as sales figures, Internet chatter, and public opinion research
proving that the vast majority of the public has not heard about
the allegation or issue and that confidence in the product is un-
deterred. In short, our crisis management program is working.

Sometimes the best opportunity to publicize your crisis
management successes is after the dust has settled. In 1993, Pepsi
was rocked by wild rumors that syringes were making their way
into Diet Pepsi cans. Starting in Seattle, this urban myth quickly
spread to other cities and—what a surprise—the news media
made matters worse by adding credibility to the accounts. To its
credit, the company never digressed into the flawed crisis management dogma that would have had them "expressing concern"
and "apologizing to the public." It was clearly a hoax and they
aggressively got out the message that there was no way on God's
green earth that you can get a syringe into a soda can. Police began to arrest people perpetuating false reports, and one person
was caught on a convenience store video surveillance camera
trying to sneak a syringe into a can. The hoax was busted.

More to the point, Pepsi afterward was none too subtle
about branding its handling of the situation a raging success.
The company ran ads nationally thanking consumers for maintaining faith in the company (even though many didn't). It also
prepared a glossy handout titled "What Went Right" that retold
events in accurate but generally favorable terms and highlighted
how Pepsi rose to the challenge and prevailed. These were all

great moves. Public perception of whether Pepsi did all the right things could easily have swung the other way. The company made sure it didn't by conducting PR for its own crisis management programs.

Granted, not every crisis is so clear cut, nor are the outcomes as conclusive as Pepsi's bout with syringe rumors. Ads and glossy brochures are probably not appropriate for 99 percent of the crises facing corporations today. However, there are several other more appropriate and targeted ways to get the word out that a crisis has been handled and put to bed. Consider placing an article in a leading trade publication respected by your industry. A top executive could recount the key facts (knocking down any residual misinformation), talk up the company's good efforts, provide some "lessons learned" to the trade, and convey a sense of closure to the whole affair. Presentations at conventions or trade shows, including sponsoring a workshop on crisis management, might be another approach. At minimum, you can make sure salespeople and other customer-facing employees are prepared with materials, talking points, and the training necessary to position the company's crisis management endeavors in the best light.

Whatever the crisis you may be facing, the primary point is that our scandal-obsessed, crisis-consuming public has become conditioned to expect a few very specific things out of whoever is on the hot seat. Call them the rituals of crisis management. Most of all, they want to see someone out there publicly explaining themselves or the company. In today's media environment, silence equals guilt. Yes, there are times when you may have to, out of necessity, hide behind a half-page statement as you scramble to get yourself together. We have counseled many a client to lay low if that is what the circumstance dictates. But if people's lives are significantly affected, or there are real health and safety risks involved, you must share with people what you know. A good crisis counselor can show you how to do that without saying more than you should.

Getting out first and characterizing the situation accurately (while avoiding liability risks) positions you as a credible, reliable player in whatever happens. If you don't, expect the crisis critics in the press, the blogosphere, Wall Street, and everywhere else to have a field day.

CHAPTER 14

Know When to Fold Them

A good retreat is better than a bad stand.

—OLD IRISH SAYING

Crisis management consulting is not without its alchemists who claim they can spin any disaster into gold. Don't be snookered. There are times when that voice screaming inside your brain *"Get out now!"* deserves an audience. While it is rarely wise to completely break ranks and run, knowing when and how to execute a strategic retreat is a survival skill well worth learning.

One such situation involved the kind of midscale burger and seafood restaurant chain found in shopping malls nationally. One of its outlets was located just blocks from a large high school, and on nights after football and basketball games it had become *the* place for students to gather. Teenagers being who they are, they would all tend to show up at once, loud and quite energized. Once seated they would move tables together and things would get a bit rowdy. Other patrons would sometimes complain. Over time, tension developed between the serving staff and the kids. The restaurant manager came to believe the trouble wasn't worth the business.

On one such night, the manager, who happened to be white, claimed she overheard one of the high school students, who happened to be black, tell a friend he had a gun. Panicked, she immediately called 911. In a nervous voice she told the police operator that a patron was armed and deadly violence could break out any moment. She also used racially derogative terms in describing the black male, which was recorded on audiotape, as all emergency calls are.

The police arrived just as the suspected gun-packing teens were exiting the restaurant. They were aggressively wrestled to the ground, handcuffed, and searched. No gun. It turned out that not only were these teens unarmed, witnesses later said the accused had never uttered a word to anyone about carrying a gun. Moreover, they were model students, had no prior record of any trouble, and were well respected among teachers and peers.

Understandably, their parents were outraged. And when they obtained, through their attorneys, a copy of the 911 recording, they went ballistic. They demanded a meeting with the local restaurant managers, who naively agreed to allow the entire discussion to be tape recorded. Had that tape ever made it into the hands of a reporter, the story would have raged for weeks, to say the least. Afterward, the parents briefed a local preacher active in city civil rights issues.

By the time this all made its way up the chain to corporate headquarters, the crisis management imperative was clear:

immediate and complete capitulation. The number two executive of the company was promptly dispatched to deliver to the wrongly accused teens and their parents the most humble and sincere apology he could muster. Plus, checkbook in hand, he literally negotiated on the spot four-year college scholarships for two of the teens, in lieu of a lawsuit and unimaginably horrible publicity. The manager was fired and other steps were taken, not the least of which were a major upgrade of the racial-sensitivity training and a complete overhaul of the firm's crisis-escalation procedures. This was no time for spin.

WHEN TO RUN

There are actually several instances where, like the restaurant chain, companies need to recognize that a major dose of acquiescence is the better part of valor.

- **When a company has clearly done something wrong.** If a clear mistake or misdeed has been committed, by all means fix it, explain your actions, apologize, and make amends. Being a responsible company requires being publicly accountable for acting in a harmful or reckless manner. Especially when the problem, the harm, and who is at fault are clear-cut—an oil spill, a chemical discharge, a deviation from corporate privacy policies, or an offensive or insensitive remark, for example.

- **When the controversy is in its infancy.** Making concessions and fostering dialogue with aggrieved parties works best early in the life cycle of controversy. Initiating conciliatory talks is a far less viable option after weeks or months of trench warfare because, over time, disputes become more about beating the other side than truly resolving differences. Moreover, negotiating from strength is far better than having been bludgeoned into submission. The time to appear magnanimous is when you have the upper hand.

- **When the agitator is a sympathetic member of a core constituency.** This is a tricky one because the suggestion here is not to roll over just because someone is evoking the persona of persecution or moral outrage. However, restraint and deftness are required when confronting allegations hurled by employees, consumers, shareholders, community members, and others who may be essential to the work of the company. Don't eat your own.

- **When the object of attack isn't worth fighting for.** Some views just aren't worth the climb, as the saying goes. In today's topsy-turvy world, even companies in the right can become the bad guy in a dispute if they appear to be bullying. A consumer wants her money back. An employee jumps to a competitor. A shareholder causes a scene at the annual meeting. A reporter from a small-town paper has written an obnoxious but relatively inconsequential article. Consider turning the other cheek. Bringing down a big corporate hammer on the little guy can bounce right back up and smack you. Save your wrath, your resources, and your reputation for when you really need them.

- **When the targeted company doesn't have an ounce of fight in them.** Let's face it, within some companies—from the CEO down to the mailroom—the culture is so timid, so bureaucratic, and so naive about "the real world" that the will to fight back is simply not there. As much as a few bold souls within the company may want to take up arms, absent strong signals from the top and a true commitment from leadership to see things through, the wiser course of action may be to settle early and often. You can't turn Bambi into Rambo.

A key challenge in all of this is making the concession soon enough to have a real impact. Corporations under fire prefer to keep their options open, and who doesn't? An often-used recommendation in strategy meetings is "Let's respond proportionally" to the threat or situation. No flying off the handle and all of that. Let's not drive the issue.

That line of thinking is all very reasonable-sounding and hard to contest. But the problem is eleventh-hour concessions ring hollow. Besides, the escalation of a crisis does not rise at a steady 45-degree angle. It can accelerate suddenly—and often unpredictably. More often than not, read-and-react is a losing paradigm.

One chemical company learned this lesson the hard way. A coalition of environmentalists was alleging that a chemical used in the manufacture of a wide range of consumer products presented a health risk. The evidence was weak. Most toxicologists will tell you that when present only at trace levels—parts per billion—most manmade chemicals aren't dangerous to people.

However, level-headed science becomes subordinated to the

emotional hot-button reactions of consumers when children are involved. The consumer uses of the chemical included products used by infants. Spooking a young mother over a scary-sounding chemical even remotely detectable in a product that may end up in their baby's mouth is not hard to do. Given the relatively small market share represented by this segment, was it wise to defend it? Yes, it's legitimate to argue that exiting a market without scientific cause would set a bad precedent. But an alternative approach would have been to deny the opposition the chance to generate widespread outrage and negative media attention by getting out early on the company's own terms. Protect larger markets by dropping a small one.

The company chose to stay the course. No efforts were made to restrict the use of this chemical in infant products. The inevitable attacks came. Mothers were terrorized. The media fanned the issue. Retailers caved. And when reports came in that infant products were being removed from store shelves in the interest of "maintaining consumer confidence," it was over. Too late now to exit under the company's own terms. The opportunity to preempt had passed.

AVOIDING BATTLES THAT AREN'T WORTH FIGHTING

Fast-food king McDonald's, a favorite target of the food consumer groups and other corporate campaigners, has over the years developed a taste for avoiding fights whenever possible. It may have started in 1990 when, under pressure from environmentalists, the company dropped the polystyrene "clamshells" used to package hamburgers and switched to paper wrapping. The environmental merits of the decision were highly questionable, but with the blessing of the Environmental Defense Fund, McDonald's chose to put the issue behind it. And so it has been over the years. Whether it is controversy over genetically modified foods, animal welfare, trans-fatty French fries, or supersized menus, the policy of McDonald's is to keep focused on selling hamburgers, not to get embroiled in crises. Even if that requires waving a white flag from time to time.

Misery likes company, and corporations about to exit a technology or market prefer to surround themselves with friends. Over the last several years, soft drink and food companies have been under increasing fire to alter the selection of products sold in schools. Soda makers in particular resisted pressure to remove their vending machines, but with growing anxiety over childhood obesity, it was a losing battle. This was a wise recognition. The PR costs of fighting to keep soft drinks in school weren't worth the business return on investment.

But instead of appearing to succumb to a collection of hectoring junk-food critics, they seized an opportunity to announce their concessions alongside the more dignified presence of former president Bill Clinton and his Clinton Initiative. While it was more of a negotiated surrender than a stunning victory, the relationship did enable these companies to prevent a rout and to establish a set of nutrition-responsibility policies on which they can build.

Citigroup stopped offering single-premium credit insurance on its mortgage loans in the face of mounting pressure by consumer advocates and government regulators who termed the practice "predatory." According to its critics, under single-premium insurance, the homeowner rolls the cost of premiums into the base of their mortgage, thereby increasing their monthly payments and foregoing the option of dropping the insurance later on.

By acting preemptively, Citigroup won the praise of the U.S. Conference of Mayors and some of its critics. They also defused momentum in the New York General Assembly to outlaw the product, which would have been a political disaster for the bank. A company spokesperson positioned the action as representative of Citigroup's commitment to "take a leadership role in raising standards and practices in the financial services industry." This was clearly a case of weighing the business value against the PR negatives, and making a levelheaded assessment to get out while the getting was good.

Looking ahead, if there is one issue that requires restraint on behalf of business and the occasional need for strategic concession it is the public's demand for privacy. Just in the last five years a host of data brokers, direct marketers, banks, credit card companies, and insurers, just to name a few, have found themselves caught in the cross fire between the lure of having access to an incredible wealth of marketing information and public outrage over having what they consider sensitive, private information about their lives and buying habits available to anyone who wants to buy it. Executives be advised: Failing to recognize the intense consumer sensitivity to certain data-mining practices is a good way to end up in front of a congressional hearing or a pack of scandal-hungry journalists.

So, if that time comes when throwing in the towel is the wisest course of action, how do you do it?

First of all, do not act so precipitously that you leave your customers and allies in the lurch. If they have been hanging in there, or standing up for you in a heated environment, they deserve to be taken care of. If possible, give them advance notice. Offer alternatives to what is being removed. Provide for an orderly transition. Many times, when there is no imminent health or safety threat, you can defuse the situation by announcing your exit sometime in the future—not abruptly, not immediately. That gives you time to do it right and to leave essential relationships intact.

Second, give careful thought to how you handle the announcement. If it is done early enough, it may not require a lot of public fanfare. There is no use in igniting an issue where there isn't one already. If it is late in the game, or if the product, practice, technology, or whatever it may be is well known, consider letting your closest, internal audiences know first. Tell the board, customers, employees, and key business partners what you plan to do, why, and how. Don't leave it for them to find out, unprepared, by reading about it in the newspaper. That would only compound their agitation. Arm them to be your advocates by educating them first.

Of course, the messaging of the announcement depends on myriad factors. It's hard to generalize. Obviously, simple and straightforward is better than evasive and complex. This doesn't mean that the language is "We're withdrawing product X due to overwhelming controversy." But entirely ignoring external pressures can reinforce the perception that the company is out of touch. Whatever is said, the themes should be focused on listening to the public, putting consumers first, and maintaining confidence in the company and its products.

Third, the measurement of an exit strategy isn't that the

problem disappears immediately. It rarely does. Detractors will claim victory and up the ante. Portions of virtually every audience won't like the terms. And any significant transition will hit snags. Success should be measured by the extent that you are able to assert your rationale at the announcement, your ability to maintain strong, your trustful relationships with your most essential audiences, and the rededication of your energies and resources back to the core mission of running a business.

CHAPTER 15

The Best Case Studies Are the Ones You'll Never Hear About

People in Washington say it's not the initial offense that gets you into trouble, it's the cover-up. They say you should admit what you did, get the story out and move on. What this overlooks is the fact that most of the time the cover-up works just fine, and nobody finds out a thing.

—GEORGE CARLIN

The study of crisis management is based upon a universe of information and opinions assembled in the form of known literature such as case histories, legal archives, and journalism. The more interesting data, however, lie in what *hasn't* been recorded, and there's a reason for that: Some of the best case studies are ones the players didn't want recorded.

The main reason many crisis survivors don't keep notes is because they don't want to remind the world of the problem. Another reason is that the truth about how a problem really disappeared often violates our sense of how the world should work.

Settlements were reached, deals were cut, and painful wrongs were quietly righted.

A CEO pays a vexatious former employee a six-figure sum to keep his observations about an embarrassing, but not illegal, corporate episode quiet; a company surreptitiously learns that an activist group that had been attacking them had been secretly supported all along by a subversive member of its own board; and a manufacturer catches a medical expert short-selling the stock of the company he's criticizing. The expert ceases his attacks, but his modus operandi is never publicized. The problem just . . . goes away.

None of these real examples will ever appear in a business school case study because, first, academics would find these methods to be in violation of their self-flagellating right-to-know dogma, and second, because it is in the best interest of the leading players to make sure it doesn't become a case study. The use of discretion to mitigate problems should not be rejected out of hand as being unethical. After all, very respectable executives have rescued their businesses by avoiding the kind of public relations spectacles that are celebrated as "well-handled crises" in an age when self-promotion is often mistaken for quality. To the contrary, in some of the best-managed crises in recent memory, discretion was the guiding principle.

PLAYING THE INSIDE GAME AT TYCO

Tyco's notorious crisis may have been operatic, but its impressive recovery spearheaded by CEO Edward Breen went largely unheralded. Despite the well-publicized collapse of companies like scandal-plagued WorldCom, Enron, and Adelphia, industrial products giant Tyco, which was looted to the tune of $600 million by convicted executives Dennis Kozlowski and Mark Swartz, never suffered a material loss of revenue in 2002–2004 when the company was under the most intense scrutiny, including the trial of Kozlowski and Swartz.

Dennis Kozlowski harbored ambitions of becoming the next Jack Welch. He took the conglomerate from $3 billion in sales in 1993 to $33 billion in 2002, an impressive Welch-like feat accomplished largely by the aggressive acquisition of a disparate collection of companies whose businesses ranged from construction to home security to disposable medical supplies. Nor was Kozlowski shy about trumpeting his success to the business press, a top priority for him. "We don't believe in perks, not even executive parking spots," Kozlowski once told *Business Week.*

Tyco shareholders, it turns out, were paying for Kozlowski's and Swartz's opulent lifestyles, including their housing, which famously featured a $6,000 shower curtain in the maid's bathroom and a $15,000 umbrella stand. Then there was the corporate-funded fortieth-birthday party Kozlowski threw for his wife in Sardinia, which featured men dressed as Roman gladiators, (barely) toga-clad model-waitresses, an ice sculpture of Michelangelo's David urinating Stolichnaya vodka, and a two-hour musical set by Jimmy Buffett billed at $250,000.

Perhaps most fortunately for Tyco, wrote *USA Today* reporter Greg Farrell in his book *America Robbed Blind,* "The accounting fraud at Tyco did not distort the company's earnings to the degree that occurred at Enron and WorldCom. Instead, the company's top executives—Kozlowski and Swartz—lavished tens of millions of dollars in bonuses on themselves that weren't disclosed to shareholders."

Furthermore, it was Tyco's board of directors that initiated action against its wayward leaders, not law enforcement. A company that alerts the authorities to malfeasance will be treated better than one that is perceived to have been "caught" by them. From the beginning, it was clear that a cabal of chieftains had engineered the fraud at Tyco, not a widely followed business model. Manhattan district attorney Robert Morgenthau charged Kozlowski and Swartz with more than 30 crimes. Farrell writes, "In an indictment, Morgenthau's office claimed that Kozlowski and Swartz had run a 'criminal enterprise.'" Their first trial was declared a mistrial, but the duo was convicted by a Manhattan jury in June 2005.

Ed Breen was hired away from Motorola to head up Tyco in the summer of 2002, shortly after Kozlowski resigned. He immediately embarked on a series of decisive operational actions. Within a month of his arrival at Tyco, Breen dismissed the entire board of directors as well as most of Kozlowski's senior management. Today 480 of 500 employees at corporate headquarters are Breen-era hires. "Many of us are more risk-taking personalities than you might find in corporate America," said Charlie Young, senior vice president of marketing and communications, who joined Tyco from General Electric. "I guess you'd have to be to leave a secure environment and go to a company that had been embroiled in controversy." Breen also appointed a senior vice president of corporate governance and put an end to Kozlowski's rampage of acquisition, unloading unprofitable businesses such as an undersea cable network.

Fortunately for Tyco, it was not a household name, and most of the company was owned by institutional investors. Since the federal government's procurement arm, the General Services

Administration, had banned government agencies from doing business with Tyco, this helped Breen focus. He would preserve the existing vulnerable government contracts that constituted much of Tyco's business, and not worry about a massive marketing offensive geared toward millions of consumers across the globe. Since many Tyco companies, such as ADT Security Services, did not bear the Tyco name, a huge rebranding program would not be necessary. It would also be easier to convey a personal touch by reassuring a handful of institutional investors instead of a huge number of angry individual investors.

Once the effort to bring Tyco's former leaders to justice was set in motion, Breen recognized that the company needed to establish its moral authority with an elite audience—institutional investors, Washington policy makers, and state governments—in order to underscore that Kozlowski-ism was no longer the operating philosophy at Tyco.

All this helped slash Tyco's debt from $28 billion to $16 billion, and increased the company's cash flow from a dangerously low $779 million in 2002 to $3.4 billion one year later. While Tyco hasn't enjoyed its Kozlowski-era stock price high of $62, it has climbed from its $8 low (when Breen took over) to $28 at this writing. In January 2006, Breen announced a plan to break up the conglomerate into three segments. "It's the best way to create long-term shareholder value at the company," Breen said. "I really stress long term, because I'm not looking for some overnight pop here."

Tyco's redemption has been one rooted in decisive business actions. The company's communications were highly targeted, focusing on tangible measures to improve fundamentals and not heartfelt promises, self-congratulation, and daydreams of a sunnier day. While there has been some news coverage of Tyco's recovery, one senses that public relations was secondary to operational results. Rightly so, and Breen has never shed his low-key businessman's demeanor. Tyco's recovery strongly suggests that favorable attention follows demonstrable performance, not vice versa.

BETTING THE INDUSTRY: HOW WIRELESS WAS SAVED FROM ATTACK

By any measurement, the great Cell Phone Scare of 1993 could have wiped out an entire industry. But it didn't.

On January 21, 1993, a man named David Reynard announced on *Larry King Live* his lawsuit against two cellular phone manufacturers. His wife had died shortly before of a brain tumor, and Reynard believed that her cellular phone caused her illness. Motorola, the largest manufacturer of cell phones, swiftly lost 20 percent of its market value. Other manufacturers were similarly hurt.

Congressional hearings were soon held to explore the potential links between cell phones and cancer. Health experts took to the airwaves to suggest ways to reduce one's cancer risk. These methods included holding the phone away from one's ear; using an earpiece, which keeps more distance between the antenna and the user; and even purchasing a special shield that insulates the head from electromagnetic waves.

The many benefits of cell phones—the convenience, the usefulness, the reliability, the affordable cost—gave millions of people a vested interest in the products' continued success. (It's worth noting that the most important factor in a product's survivability is how badly the consumer needs it.) While many were anxious about the possibility that cell phones caused cancer, the public was searching for any evidence that could be produced to the contrary.

And that evidence is exactly what consumers got.

The wireless industry's trade group, the Cellular Telecommunications and Internet Association (CTIA), created an independent research body expressly devoted to examining potential cause and effect between cell phones and cancer. Called the Wireless Technology Research (WTR) group, it received $25 million in funding from the industry. To conduct its research and ensure its credibility, it used Government Accounting Office guidelines. Furthermore, the Harvard Center for Risk Analysis at the School of Public Health convened a panel of independent scientists.

Over a five-year period, the WTR sponsored more than 50 studies and found no clear hazardous link. Said Tom Wheeler, then CEO of CTIA:

> The substantial body of scientific evidence on possible health effects from RF [radio frequency] does not indicate a link between the use of wireless phones and adverse health effects. Scientific conclusions are not based upon one study alone, but rather on an entire body of research and in this case the weight of scientific evidence continues to reaffirm that there are no adverse health effects from the use of wireless phones.

In 1993, the time of the initial scare, there were 13 million cell phone subscribers. (Today there are 194 million.) Not only were cell phones popular by 1993, there had been no reputable evidence at the time linking them with cancer. The industry thus had enough confidence in its products to swiftly and generously fund WTR, and that won them extraordinary credibility with the government. Indeed, in 1999 the Food and Drug Administration said of the WTR studies, "We didn't see what we thought were public heath problems."

The Federal Communications Commission, working closely with CTIA, developed guidelines about the energy emitted from cell phones. CTIA announced in December 2000 that all new wireless phones would come with consumer information about absorption rates.

The industry had decided upon a blue-chip, science-based response to manage the crisis, recognizing early the dangers of "overcommunicating," which could unnecessarily trigger concerns among an already anxious public by talking about things that were poorly understood. One main voice of crisis communications, CTIA, was assigned responsibility. This was no small feat since the number one challenge in confronting industry-wide crises is the inability to establish leadership for fear of ruffling political feathers. What often results is a hypersensitive confederacy more committed to gaining democratic input on how a battle should be managed than to defeating a common enemy.

CTIA anchored its measured outreach in well-funded scientific research that was intentionally designed to go beyond the scope of "publicity science"—token studies implemented on the cheap in order to feed a clamoring media. The organization forged a successful working relationship with government regulators, emphasizing a core group of influential decision makers over mass communications, and communicated only when it had something to say, such as when there were scientific results, and when there was a likelihood of third-party support either from the WTR or the federal government.

Many science- and technology-based industries wrongly assume that the public will evaluate a scare with an analytical eye. But reason and crisis management rarely meet. Damage control is a slugfest of emotions, and the mega-billion-dollar wireless industry turned out to have had marketing instincts as savvy as its technological prowess. Cell phone manufacturers resisted institutional denial and recognized the gravity of the situation it had on its hands. Its leadership, committed to the marketplace for the long haul, moved swiftly to demonstrate that its products were safe, but not so swiftly that the foundation couldn't produce a program of enduring value.

CHAPTER 16

In Crisis, Personality Trumps Planning

Though he had always been a careful planner, life on the frontier had long ago convinced him of the fragility of plans. The truth was, most plans did fail, to one degree or another, for one reason or another. He had survived as a Ranger because he was quick to respond to what he had actually found, not because his planning was infallible.

—ON CAPTAIN WOODROW CALL, FROM LARRY
MCMURTRY'S *LONESOME DOVE*

After Hurricanes Katrina and Rita lashed the Gulf Coast in 2005, media pundits were united on one point: What the victims of these natural disasters needed was . . . a good plan. The demand for a plan was also a routine complaint when there were setbacks in the war in Iraq.

Whenever bad news strikes, whether it's an act of God or a product recall, the airwaves are full of experts diving in front of cameras to express outrage that [insert scapegoat] didn't have a plan.

Here we are, the most sophisticated people in the history of civilization, and we don't have a strategic plan for everything? After all, we're certainly aware of the constant demand for plans. Could it be that someone very clever has "the" plan (Hurricane-B-Gone, TidyWar), but keeps it hidden? Or is there an obvious plan that we're too incompetent to implement?

Our collective plan-worship is as absurd as waiting for Godot. Here's the harsh reality: All the planning in the world doesn't address the reality that God, Faith, Fortune, Lady Luck—name your belief system—has reviewed your crisis management plan and will make sure to visit a scenario upon you that wasn't anticipated.

Strategic planning, to be fair, can be a valuable exercise, but too many businesses and institutions view "strategy" as a utopian stand-in for what's really needed in a crisis, and that's leadership. Even the most banal ideas take on a whiff of gravitas when the word "strategic" is added into the mix.

The world doesn't run on strategies; it runs on emotions—egos, biases, passions, dreams, jealousies, resentments, gut reactions. Most corporations under siege devote far too much attention to strategy and not enough on the key personalities.

Political scientists and social psychologists are starting to recognize the canyon that separates why people *believe* they vote for a candidate (or like a person) and the real reasons they do. The essence is this: People follow—or reject—*people,* not rationally processed analyses. It comes down to a pairing of personality and climate. In other words: Do we like you in the context of the challenge at hand?

When we are retained to work on a crisis or marketplace assault, our immediate interest is in meeting our client's leader and assessing his or her personality. We are not looking for flamboyance; we are looking at the character of the person in charge: Is this individual a consensus builder? A maverick? Does the leader appear to have a long-term vision, or does he view himself as a temporary custodian?

The main criterion for a strong leader in crisis situations is a capacity for making decisions. The cornerstone of good decision-making judgment is an appreciation of realistic options. Too many crisis teams are paralyzed by dream scenarios proposed to them by consultants.

A case in point: We once worked with a petrochemical company that failed to address criticism about the safety of its product because the crisis team's leader couldn't focus on anything but winning environmentalists' approval. No matter how many times we told our client, "They [environmentalists] just don't like you, and they never will," the client held on to his delusion, which distracted him and cost the company valuable response time.

Another feature of good leadership is the willingness to make decisions based upon incomplete information. In crises, organizations never feel they have sufficient information. But the marketplace doesn't forgive inaction for any reason. Good leaders will take calculated risks with the understanding that there are no guarantees their decisions will be right. Rendering judgments on the fly is especially relevant in an age of fast-breaking news.

If given the choice between a thorough plan and a good leader, go with the leader, because people rarely separate the event from the personalities that dominate the event.

When the twin towers of the World Trade Center fell on 9/11, Mayor Rudy Giuliani didn't have a plan. But he earned goodwill because of his personality. Defense Secretary Donald Rumsfeld received favorable news coverage when he held regular news conferences during the successful overthrow of the Taliban in Afghanistan. When Diet Pepsi cans were rumored to be spiked with syringes in 1993, the visible activism of the soft drink's chief Craig Weatherup played a role in reassuring consumers that safety-minded people were at the company's helm. (Remember Coca-Cola's disastrous standoffishness?)

The contrast between the understated Ed Breen and the vulgar Dennis Kozlowski helped send the right message to the stakeholders in Tyco's recovery, which was that redemption would come via a low-key focus on the company's fundamentals.

The sheer difference in the personal style of GE's Jeffrey Immelt from that of his predecessor, Jack Welch, helped defuse expectations that Immelt would "out-Welch" Welch.

And sometimes the character of the individual in charge of the crisis becomes synonymous with the crisis management strategy.

"MR. CLEAN" CONFRONTS THE ULTIMATE MARKETPLACE ASSAULT

When waste hauler Browning-Ferris Industries (BFI) moved into the New York City garbage market in 1993, one of their top executives found the severed head of a German shepherd on his front lawn. A note stuffed in the dog's mouth read "Welcome to New York."

There was little doubt about the provenance of this "welcome": A Mafia cartel had monopolized waste hauling in New York City for decades at extortionate rates and didn't want competition from corporate BFI. Carting was a $1.5 billion business in New York; two-thirds of that figure was the mob's "tax" on services.

BFI faced a stark choice: Stay or leave New York. If BFI's corporate strategy was to enter lucrative new markets, CEO William D. Ruckelshaus reasoned, BFI would not be bullied out of New York. The company's response was a direct function of the character of the man leading BFI.

Ruckelshaus was mobster John Gotti's polar opposite. Tall, square-jawed, and soft-spoken, the Indiana-bred Ruckelshaus had been the first administrator of the U.S. Environmental Protection Agency, where he was dubbed "Mr. Clean," and was acting director of the FBI. He had also resigned during Watergate's infamous "Saturday Night Massacre," which occurred when Ruckelshaus and his then-boss, Attorney General Elliot Richardson, refused to fire special prosecutor Archibald Cox at President Nixon's command.

"People have so little trust these days in our government institutions. That really bothers me," said Ruckelshaus at the time of the New York crisis.

Said Philip Angell, who was Ruckelshaus's deputy at both the EPA and BFI:

If we believed that eventually the [New York] market would be opened and the organized crime taint expunged, the fact that we were the first and only national company to do that would redound to our benefit not only in New York City, but elsewhere in the country as we bid for public and private contracts alike. Since it seemed common knowledge nationwide that the trash industry was linked in some way with the mob, if we were seen as helping to change that, it could do nothing but enhance our reputation."

Immediately after the dog head incident, Ruckelshaus and Angell rushed to New York to meet with concerned employees. Ruckelshaus reaffirmed his commitment to the market and offered BFI salespeople the incentive of a year's free housing if they would move to New York. In the months ahead, representatives of the gangland-controlled cartel paid visits to customers that had signed on with BFI (at savings of 30 to 60 percent compared to cartel prices). Suspiciously, many of these customers cancelled their contracts with BFI despite their savings. Others, like Citicorp, whose carting fees BFI offered to drop by 40 percent, didn't sign with BFI for fear of gangland retaliation.

As BFI continued to offer potential customers better carting deals, a full-fledged crisis management program was in the works. The program included an extensive compilation of intimidation incidents and an agreement with the Manhattan district attorney's office to assist them in a sweeping investigation of the mob-dominated carting cartel, which included placing an undercover agent within BFI's ranks. "The one thing these mob guys can't survive is exposure," said Angell, Ruckelshaus's point man in New York.

BFI began running print advertisements in the New York marketplace drawing attention to—not shying away from—the limited choices businesses faced. One ad featured a photograph of a tough-looking face on the page, along with a tagline reading "Until Now Your Waste Disposal Options Were Somewhat Limited." The message was clear: We all know who dominates waste hauling in New York, but there's a new player in town.

The cartel, through a trade association, hit back, alleging that the advertisements were a slur against Italian Americans. They took out their own ads listing BFI's own environmental violations and run-ins with the law. Ruckelshaus as "Mr. Clean" stood his ground, giving a round of interviews in New York–area publications hammering his mob-busting message.

"He's a guy with some guts," District Attorney Morgenthau said of Ruckelshaus, whose law enforcement pedigree was reassuring to the DA. Ruckelshaus, in turn, said, "I trust Morgenthau implicitly. You don't have to talk to him long to see what a determined man he is to root out crime in New York City in his seventies."

What resulted from this partnership was one of the biggest investigations ever undertaken by the New York Police Department and the Manhattan district attorney, according to *Fortune* magazine, including "ten assistant DAs on the case, raids by 500 cops on 26 locations, more than 3,000 hours of electronic surveillance, even a videotape showing physical threats made to a driver for a rival carter who was beaten within a hair of his life with planks and baseball bats."

DA Morgenthau's "Operation Wasteland" put a number of garbage godfathers in maximum security prisons. A decade after the raids by law enforcement, BFI (since acquired by Allied Waste Systems) remains in the New York marketplace, but so do other national carters that benefited from BFI's risk taking.

Smaller, local companies with no ties to organized crime are also thriving. The mob's hold on carting has been crippled, the new generation of racketeers being less adept than their predecessors at influencing legitimate enterprise. The annual savings to New York City has been estimated at $500 million to $640 million.

Wrote *Fortune* of Ruckelshaus as the BFI drama unfolded, "[Ruckelshaus] is at least exceptionally brave and could end up looking canny."

CHAPTER 17

Know Whose Side Your Team Is On

Results are often obtained by impetuosity and daring which could neverhave been obtained by ordinary methods.

—NICCOLO MACHIAVELLI

Central to the notion of crisis management is the idea of a high-tech war room complete with huge blinking maps and hypercompetent specialists who can retrieve obscure data from around the globe with the click of a mouse. Think Kiefer Sutherland's Counterterrorism Unit in the hit Fox TV program *24*.

The reality: When a crisis hits, you will feel an Alice in Wonderland sense of having fallen into a hole only to encounter strange creatures who mean you harm. In a crisis, you feel alone. You feel betrayed. You are in a state of disbelief, having never predicted that *this* would be your crisis. Is the outcome of this situation destined to be my legacy, you wonder?

In crisis, you are at the mercy of something larger than yourself. You vaguely recall reading an article in an airline magazine about this type of situation. The article contained suggestions that made sense at the time. *Tell the truth. Express concern. Apologize.* Now none of these suggestions appears to have any application to your situation, and you begin to wonder about the real-world experience of the attractive person whose photo appeared next to the byline.

You will reach out frantically for experts—lawyers and consultants—and may find yourself angry with them that they have no easy answers. As the days go by, however, you will unconsciously begin to cherish one trait in the people you have around you: old-fashioned loyalty, that intangible sense that someone close by is on your side, the conviction that you are not, in fact, alone.

In crisis situations, people do what they know, not necessarily what's right. What people know is tied very closely to who they are. Crises are traumatic, so while the organization's strategic objective may be problem solving, the individual's imperative is comfort. Some are discreetly updating and circulating their résumés. Others may be leaking confidential information to the press. Some are angling to hire consultants who will counsel actions that will be the least likely to put their sponsors at risk.

In a desire to ensure a return to normalcy, those in crisis demand complete information, which is understandable but often futile. Such folly sometimes comes in the form of calls for more public opinion research. Complete information usually isn't coming, and the demand for it simply delays the onset of decisive leadership. Action, you will find, needs to be taken based on good judgment, not perfect information.

Executives' ability to confront challenges is hampered by the "clean" notion of crisis and recovery, as if there is an end state, a singular moment when victory can be declared. The reality is that most issues are chronic—product safety, union tensions, activist boycotts—and don't lend themselves to fairy-tale endings. More often than not, once the acute phase of a crisis ends, a period of coping or adaptation begins.

Affluent—and blessed—societies like ours demand order and certainty. We've had it so good for so long that anything that inconveniences us strikes us as a screwup on somebody's part. The Watergate-era battle cry—What did the president know and when did he know it?—is hyperapplied to contingencies within and beyond the control of humankind. Americans especially don't believe in acts of God; there is only negligence, usually corporate. With this mind-set, the antidote to chaos can be something that only humans, in their infinite wisdom, have engineered.

THE PLAYERS

There are few things more politically incorrect and socially offensive than making sweeping generalizations about types of people; after all, the contemporary notion is that we are each unique snowflakes who cannot be categorized. Perhaps, but isn't it also safe to say that all snowflakes are frozen and white?

There are four career categories that tend to come into play in crisis situations: PR people; leaders, who may be business unit chiefs or CEOs; lawyers; and technical experts. Each of these players brings assets and liabilities to the crisis team. Whether individuals choose careers or careers choose individuals, there are certain attributes that these players tend to have in common. Understanding, in practical terms, their DNA going into the

cial to understanding the counsel they offer,
:t the outcome of a crisis.

In his famous essay "The Hedgehog and the Fox," historian-philosopher Isaiah Berlin divides intellectuals into foxes, who believe events are caused by a complex collision of often invisible forces, and hedgehogs, who believe that a central organizing principle governs human events. Wrote the Greek poet Archilochus, "The fox knows many things, but the hedgehog knows one very big thing."

Like the hedgehog, which survives by its core skill of dissuading attackers by showing its quills, public relations people tend to embrace a singular dogma: *Events are communications problems* that can be addressed with a prescription of "positive messaging"; soft-focus advertisements; "dialogue" with one's adversaries; and, of course, the mea culpa as panacea.

PR people are at their best when anticipating how important audiences are going to react to the deployment of particular strategies and messages. A good PR person will design communications that will have the desired effect. Internal corporate PR people are also effective playing a key role in the crisis team's synthesis—being responsible for the internal and external "plumbing" of a crisis operation.

Red flag: PR people are at their worst when confronting conflicts. Folks who go into PR tend to be "people persons"—diplomats—for whom getting along is the endgame. This is a positive attribute in holding a crisis team together, but it tends to limit the strategies that are considered for use, often ruling out anything that is considered offensive or confrontational.

This is fine when a company is culpable in its crisis, and conventional, more placating, measures are called for. Discomfort with conflict, however, becomes a problem when the company is forced into litigation or to confront critics.

Agreeability—the illusion that there are no conflicts, just misunderstandings—is in the DNA of most public relations people whose jobs have focused on projecting positive images versus the dicey game of making bad situations a little less bad. Deceit often follows desperation; the desire for affairs to return to normalcy fosters a demand for programs that mitigate conflict rather than solve problems.

All consultants are ultimately loyal to their own businesses. Conventional PR firms are seeking franchise clients—companies that will keep coming back, and paying. One way to achieve this is to palliate anxious clients with "soft" tactics—opinion research, strategic plans, training sessions—that provide the illusion that action is being taken. The tacit objective is to avoid risk, and to do it by using smart-looking props. To be sure, some of these tactics have their place, but nobody ever researched their way out of a pickle. Our experience, however, has been that at some point a decision to conduct more research is a de facto decision to filibuster, if not surrender.

Leaders

The best crisis team leaders are chief executives or business unit managers who value judgment over information. Effective crisis managers are Isaiah Berlin's foxes, who believe *events emerge from conflicts,* and that what works well to promote shampoo may fail miserably when Greenpeace alleges that the active ingredient in that shampoo is a carcinogen. With conflicts, agendas trump facts. Greenpeace *wants* that ingredient to be a carcinogen, which presents a larger problem than science can resolve.

Every time a case is complete, a crisis manager's "bag of tricks" must be returned to the shelf because the technique that helped effectively serve Acme Copper Mines during a boom economy in peacetime won't help us with the Global Software Company in a recession when the country is at war.

A good leader is impatient. He is capable of listening to alternative positions, but understands that at some point, crisis management is about mitigating pain, not guaranteeing that all voices are heard.

Leaders can have serious vulnerabilities. One of the greatest catalysts for disaster is "bubble-itis." Corporate jets, a private elevator, a secluded room at a restaurant: all are sought-after perks that are sometimes necessary to shield a subject from multitudes of grasping fans and the time-eating inefficiencies of flyover America. The problem with this is that when a subject goes from a Gulfstream V airplane to a limousine to a catered meeting to a four-star hotel, he lives in an artificial bubble of constant, uncritical reinforcement. He becomes a demigod who is a consumer of reassuring clichés, not life's friction.

In the bubble, the subject doesn't just *think* he can do anything, he *can* do anything. The bubble contains no traffic lights, no inclement weather, and no Greek chorus warning of tribulation. The most important qualification for being inside the subject's bubble is the capacity to consistently deliver the right answer: You betcha!

The ideal leader has experienced failure.

Lawyers

The lawyer's job is to keep his client out of trouble by minimizing risk. In a crisis situation, that often means keeping his client quiet. Silence may be golden in context of legal entanglements, but public dramas often require dialogue.

The lawyer will be concerned if a company says anything that implies responsibility for the problem at hand. Conveyance of responsibility may be relevant in an eventual court battle. A product recall, for example, sends a legal message: We believe there is something wrong with our product to the degree that we had to remove it from the marketplace.

The greatest tension in a crisis management war room is often between the lawyer, who tends to counsel silence, and the PR person, who wants the company to talk. The arbiter in the battle between legal conservatism and communications liberalism must be the leader. A good leader recognizes that both the lawyer and the communicator are correct within the context of their disciplines, but that a decision in one direction or the other must ultimately be made.

Technical Experts

There must be someone at the crisis table who understands the technical aspects of what's happening. In the late 1980s, we had a client that made plastics. At the time, plastics were being savagely criticized for not breaking down in landfills the way, say, paper did.

At this time, all the media and consumers wanted to talk about was biodegradability—the notion that materials break down after being discarded—and that this was, in fact, a good thing. Our science expert was furious: "You can't just make trash disappear!" he insisted. "Besides," he said, "when materials break down, they become toxic. We don't *want* our trash to break down!"

Technically, he was correct. Trash didn't just vanish. In fact, in landfills, garbage tended to mummify, and not break down. The problem was that the public believed in biodegradability; people *wanted* trash to just break down and disappear.

We faced a dilemma that frequently surfaces in war rooms: We had a scientist who was factually correct, but who would not—or could not—explain the science to the consumer public. Furthermore, he erroneously believed that science would be the vindicating factor in a marketplace where emotion reigns supreme.

Science matters in public opinion battles. But so do consumer perceptions of science. The more the plastics industry tried to explain that biodegradability wasn't the answer, the angrier the public became. While there was no silver-bullet answer, ultimately the public began seeing the facts firsthand, with the help of a landfill archaeologist, thirty-year-old newspapers, and equally dated hot dogs and carrots. At the same time plastics manufacturers were educating the public about the limits of biodegradability, plastics-recycling technology was advancing. Put differently, while expectations of biodegradability were diminishing, consumers were learning more about the promise of recycling.

Translating the wisdom of experts for the public is fundamental in many crisis situations, ranging from medical controversies (when people want to be assured they're safe) to high-stakes litigation (when juries want to decide if the defendant did or did not do it). It's not enough to have an expert who understands the technical aspects of the situation; the team must have the capacity to communicate it in a way that's personally relevant.

A WORD ABOUT DREAM TEAMS

Human nature gets interesting when the crisis team is assembled. Despite media portrayals of omniscient "dream teams"—the best talent from every specialty group—the reality is that crisis teams are nightmares. Even worse is when the company believes in having several experts from a particular discipline at the table on the grounds that the more brains, the better. Nothing could be further from the truth. While politeness often reigns in the boardroom, power struggles break out when the meeting adjourns, as executives attempt to seize—or dodge—the limelight. The foundations for blame are set.

Vendors squabble as each specialist lobbies to have his product or service employed. Pollsters want to poll, advertising executives want to advertise. PR firms want to do media tours (provided they are not forced into uncomfortable confrontations with the journalists they work with on a regular basis). Lobbyists want to set up meetings with government officials, but are reticent to go to war against those they need for other clients. More often than will be acknowledged, disgruntled vendors or employees will leak sensitive documents (such as the confidential proposals of competing firms) to investigative reporters. Just because you hired them, it doesn't mean they're on your side. Meetings drag on interminably as the leader feels compelled, in a fit of open-mindedness, to give all opinions equal weight.

KNOW WHOSE SIDE *YOU'RE* ON

You cannot advise an individual or institution to do something that goes beyond their constitution. At the beginning of a crisis or marketplace assault, emotions run high. They can range from grandiose fantasies of easily vanquishing enemies to a sense of impending catastrophe. Once these emotions settle, it will be essential to come to an understanding of what your constitution will permit you to do.

Consider the following metaphor about a child and a schoolyard bully. Many a sensitive child can recall being told to "hit him back." The problem with this counsel is that it does not factor in the nature of the child. Chances are, if a sensitive child hits back, the bully will throttle him. Better options might be to avoid the bully, attempt to befriend him, or help him with his homework. Sometimes crisis management is about making the best of your bad options.

Our portfolio of experience is replete with examples where an ultraconservative corporation will like the idea of fighting back against a critic. But the moment those ideas are converted into proposed tactics, the decision makers balk and ask to "take a few steps back" to "reexamine strategy." While there is nothing wrong with questioning decisions, companies would be well served to be realistic from the start about what they are capable of doing when an attack hits.

CHAPTER 18

The Crisis in Your Future

The trouble with our times is that the future is not what it used to be.

—PAUL VALÉRY

Crisis management is chiefly the art of dealing with the insistent "now" of a pressing problem or issue. These pages preach the value of quick thinking and strong leadership over mind-numbing scenario planning. But this doesn't mean that savvy companies and the people entrusted with protecting them shouldn't be looking around the bend. In a crisis, an understanding of the prevailing culture, context, and societal expectations can determine success or failure. Executives need to know—or at least have an educated guess about—what awaits them in the years ahead. Here are ten key trends that are shaping tomorrow's crisis environment.

1. Corporate mission creep

    Milton Friedman's famous assertion that "the business of
    business is business," not to self-consciously make the world
    a better place, is out of vogue in corporate boardrooms, and
    many would argue is no longer even on the table. Compa-
    nies of all types, but especially the large multinationals, are
    committing to a host of social, civic, health, and environ-
    mental responsibilities that far exceed following the law and
    maximizing shareholder value. For heavy industries, such as
    chemicals and energy, these commitments are de rigueur,
    and it is arguable that they help preclude unwanted regula-
    tion and grow new markets. For global goliaths like Micro-
    soft, GE, and IBM, it is imperative that they be perceived as
    societal problem solvers. But determining where this ever-
    expanding corporate responsibility stops is getting fuzzier
    and fuzzier. Does responsibility for "solving the obesity cri-
    sis" lie with overindulging and lethargic consumers or with
    food and beverage companies? Who is responsible for creat-
    ing public infrastructure in developing nations—the gov-
    ernment or the foreign companies extracting their resources?
    Are pharmaceutical companies in business to make new
    medicines or to reverse Africa's AIDS epidemic? David Hen-
    derson of London's Institute of Economic Affairs warns, "It
    is not through transforming enterprise goals and conduct,
    in the ways suggested by CSR [corporate social responsibil-
    ity] adherents, that the business contribution to the general
    welfare can be improved, but through actions by govern-
    ments that would serve to reinforce the primary role of
    business." In the coming years, crisis managers will need to

multitask across the sometimes contradictory goals of defining and promoting the company's contributions to the public good while assuring that the true engine of prosperity and quality of life—free markets—are allowed to flourish.

2. The demise of science

Science was once the domain of ivy-walled institutions and government test labs. The "scientific method"—the studious process of formulating a theory, testing it against hard metrics, and submitting it to a rigorous review by independent peers—meant everything. And, until fairly recently, when a silver-haired scientist in a white lab coat went on TV to say product X was safe, then it was safe. No more. In the future, anyone with a test tube and a blog will claim scientific standing. Special-interest groups will work with private labs to release their own findings, bypassing the once-hallowed process of peer review and journal publication. Long-established scientific institutions, of course, won't disappear, but they will be intellectually downsized—just one voice in a sea of never-ending dissension. Risk-benefit assessment—the process of weighing the evidence of potential harm against the societal benefits of a product or practice—will take a backseat to the Precautionary Principle, the "better safe than sorry" movement. Industry-aligned scientists—indeed, any type of corporately funded research—will per se be deemed tainted and suspect simply because of their association with "profit-driven business." Already, "medical silencing" tactics range from Web sites "outing" researchers who have worked with industry, to violent threats directed at scientists involved with animal testing, to new policies at scientific journals barring research submissions from anyone receiving money from corporations. "Sound science" was for many years the one arena where business could take its case and win on the facts. In the future, don't count on it.

3. Outspent and outgunned

As recently as 20 years ago, large companies could easily outspend whatever opposition they were facing: Hire the best lobbyists, best lawyers, and best PR people, and a favorable deal will be cut somehow. In the future, the opposite will be true. Already, environmental nongovernmental organizations (NGOs) alone have billions of dollars in assets, with the top ten exceeding $3 billion in collective revenues. According to one NGO watchdog, the top 13 U.S. and European NGOs boast nearly 20 million members and 162 offices across every continent. The trial bar, enriched by massive tobacco, silicon breast implant, and asbestos settlements (among others), has also amassed a war chest well into the tens of billions of dollars, which enables it to fund surrogate attacks on business and invest heavily in profitable relationships with state attorneys general, legislators, and public officials at all levels of government. Throw in the unions, which are focusing their wealth and talent less on organizing than on launching "corporate campaigns" designed to achieve concessions by turning public and media sentiment against targeted companies, and it is clear that, in terms of money and influence, the balance of power is shifting. David will become Goliath.

4. Is Junior covering your crisis?

The news media of the future will be characterized by too
few reporters with too little training chasing too many stories. And more and more businesses will be burned in the
process. Why? Because money—not public service journalism—is king in newsrooms today. It started when big companies such as General Electric, Disney, and Time Warner
bought NBC, ABC, and CNN, respectively, and turned up the
pressure to transform news reporting into a profit-making
enterprise. Once considered to be treasured (and pampered)
jewels in the corporate portfolio, news executives were ordered
to make a buck for the company like everyone else. Concur-
rently, massive changes in consumer lifestyles and technology via the Internet were swiftly reshaping how people got
their news. As a result, network TV audiences, as well as daily
newspaper readership, are shrinking rapidly. Fewer viewers
and readers mean less advertising revenue. Less revenue
means less money to pay experienced, generally older reporters and to cover the costs of dispatching news crews.
Fewer, younger, and less experienced reporters, and less
money available to thoroughly research stories, will increasingly result in stories that are quickly and poorly reported
and done primarily because they are cheap, easy to do, and
visual. And this will create enormous opportunities for
mischief, misrepresentation, and malfeasance because someone has the video and a story too expensive and too time-
consuming to check out.

5. Wall Street war zone

"Follow the money" has long been a truism for anyone tracking politics or the affairs of business. In the future, crises and controversies will increasingly follow the money to Wall Street. First of all, it is not lost on business detractors that access to capital is the lifeblood of business. Shut that access down and a corporation suffocates. This vulnerability has also not been lost on animal-rights extremists who, through violence and intimidation, have gone after Wall Street bankers and traders and already demonstrated they can make them back off from doing business with animal-research firms. Wall Street is also "going green," embracing environmentally sound investment funds. One major investment bank has retained the Rainbow Action Network— no friend to chemical, timber, and resource-extraction industries—to advise it on environmental issues. With some 50 percent of Americans owning some type of stock, even if only through mutual funds, the views, behavior, and influence of Wall Street will push it further and further into the crisis management spotlight in the coming decades.

6. Everyone's a pundit

Of course, no discussion of the future is complete without a nod to the Internet and its teeming horde of bloggers. And it is hard not to buy in to the hyperbole that "The Mainstream Media" is dead or dying, to be replaced by thousands of pajama-clad computer jockeys opining from their home offices. The stunning power of bloggers to bring down Dan

Rather and Trent Lott, or drive the ascension of presidential candidate Howard Dean, cannot be denied. But it can be overstated. What is clear is that punditry—including punditry on breaking crises—has been democratized. As InstaPundit's Glenn Reynolds has observed, "Millions of Americans who were once in awe of the punditocracy now realize that anyone can do this stuff—and that many unknowns can do it better than the lords of the profession." So, within hours, if not sooner, of your crisis going public, assume that the blogosphere will be on you like a swarm of angry bees. Indeed, InstaPundit's tongue-in-cheek slogan is "Ahead of the curve since 30 minutes ago." But as Christine Rosen, a fellow at the Ethics and Public Policy Center, counters, "Blogosphere, at its worse, values timeliness over thought . . . it's nothing more than old-fashioned techno-utopianism to assume that the blogosphere could adequately supersede the old media order [and] to believe that traditional institutions can be easily and casually jettisoned." Blogging will continue to be an influential and, at times, decisive voice in the public debate about business crises and controversy. But it will add to and not supplant the still dominant Mainstream Media.

7. Make 'em laugh

Forty years ago, the news was delivered via the gray pages of daily newspapers and the somber baritone voices of Edward R. Murrow and Walter Cronkite. Today large chunks of the American public are getting their news from comedians. And that's no joke. Far more young people are watch-

ing *The Daily Show with Jon Stewart, The Colbert Report,* or
Real Time with Bill Maher than any of the evening network
news reports. The place where ambitious politicians announce their run for office, or scandalized celebrities go to
roll out their redemption tours, is not the mainstream press
but Jay Leno or David Letterman. It is the latest installment
in the continued blurring between news and entertainment.
And it raises the question of not only what is fact and what
is satire, but to what extent viewers even care about the distinction. However, only in the rarest of cases will these forums represent opportunities for corporations to "get their
messages out." For good reason, perhaps, companies are
notoriously bad at humor. Only the hippest of executives
would feel comfortable in these formats, and they'd better
be prepared for the host and audience to laugh at them, not
with them. More likely, these shows will continue to provide
a crude but telling barometer as to how deeply a corporate
crisis has worked its way into the public consciousness. As
Newsweek's Gloria Borger has put it, the trajectory of today's
gaffes is from "YouTube, to the *Washington Post,* to a punch
line on the late-night shows." If they're laughing at your crisis, that's about as bad as it can get.

8. **Your brand is a target**

The power of today's most prominent brands will increasingly become a two-way street. Big companies spend millions and sometimes several years "brand building," and the
result is a name, symbol, or icon that is meaningful to con-

sumers, reinforces key benefits, and is rec/
wide. To some businesses, their brands are
uable assets. They can also quickly become liabilities ...
anticorporate campaigners have discovered that the best
way to promote their issues is to associate them with a well-
known brand. Concerned over the outsourcing of U.S. manufacturing jobs overseas? Attack Nike. Have a beef with
hormones in meat? Protest McDonald's. Angry over global
warming policies? Boycott ExxonMobil. And it's not just
corporate brands that are under attack. Product brands also
are targeted. Environmental groups targeted Teflon cook-
ware to generate controversy about an industrial chemical
used by DuPont and several other manufacturers. Conservative groups called on their supporters to stop buying Crest
toothpaste over objections to Procter & Gamble's advertisements in gay publications. Experience varies widely regard-
ing how much impact these so-called naming and shaming
campaigns actually have. It happens on occasion, but rarely
is the impact on product sales and share price significant
over the long haul. More typically, where they really hurt is
customer relations; employee morale; the ability to recruit
young, liberal-minded college graduates; and the corporate
costs of dealing with the negative publicity. In the future,
corporate and product brands will increasingly need to cou-
ple their promotional campaigns with brand-defense programs to mitigate efforts to turn a high-profile asset into a
platform for conflict.

9. Protecting intellectual property

Software, entertainment, and pharmaceuticals. Three massive, high-growth industries in which the United States still maintains a world leadership position. Three knowledge-based sectors where the proprietary science, engineering, and creativity that goes into the development of products is far more valuable than their easily copied output—be it a pill, a download, or a DVD. It would seem a no-brainer that, at a minimum domestically, and even abroad, both government decision makers and the public would appreciate that everyone is well served when intellectual property is respected and protected. Not so. First, all three of these types of products are relatively easy and cheap to manufacture. Illegally copying a song or movie, or sharing software, takes a matter of minutes. Second, people tend to view theft against big corporations as victimless crimes. No one sheds a tear when big business is ripped off. Third, in an "open source" culture, defined primarily by a free and unregulated Internet, a whole new generation is used to getting something for nothing. In a world where the public, media, and activists perceive a stark and heart-wrenching gap between the "haves and have-nots," companies in these businesses and others will be increasingly pressured to share their knowledge at a reduced return. The highest level of communications savvy will be required to draw the distinction between an appropriate degree of altruism and killing the golden goose.

10. The porous corporation

As much as this book focuses on external threats to a corporation, attacks from within can be equally devastating. It's hard to admit, but your own employees can sometimes be your worst enemies. Traditionally, this has tended to take three forms: the "thief," who steals secrets or cavorts with competitors; the "whistleblower," often a disgruntled employee who is lionized in the media for "exposing injustice" but is motivated chiefly by the millions he or she will receive for running to federal officials; the "kiss and tell" manager who pens a business book or sits down with *Forbes* to spin his or her tenure at the top. The future, however, will increasingly feature a new character, the "digital busybody." Whether its through a personal blog, their MySpace conversations, their YouTube video, or simply posting sensitive corporate documents on the Internet, their 15 minutes of fame will be achieved by way of their secretive acts of outing their employers. If you thought e-mail created confidentiality issues, you ain't seen nothing yet! Already, executives are complaining that their supposed confidential presentations are being discussed by industry bloggers before the meeting is over—literally. A brave new world, indeed.

The pressure all these trends—and many others—will place on large, highly visible companies will likely lead to a new type of crisis manager. We are already seeing the emergence of a standing corporate troubleshooter. Their titles vary, and they are less and less likely to come from PR departments. More often they are a lawyer by training or have deep experience in politics. Their mission is not so much to improve the company's mission but to avoid problems before they occur or to know how to make them go away as fast as possible. Call it damage control.

CHAPTER 19

Fighting Back in the Age of YouTube: The Duke Lacrosse Counteroffensive and A Roundup of Recent Crises

I guess I'd say, with a smile on my face, "Mister Nifong, you've picked on the wrong families. You've picked on the wrong families that you've indicted; you've picked on the wrong family of the Duke lacrosse team. You've picked on the wrong family of Duke University, and you will pay every day for the rest of your life."

—RAE EVANS, MOTHER OF DAVID EVANS, DUKE LACROSSE PLAYER ACCUSED OF SEXUAL ASSAULT

THE DUKE LACROSSE CASE: NAILING THE PROSECUTOR

The landmark crisis of 2007 is the saga of three members of the Duke University lacrosse team whose passionate counter-offensive against false rape charges should replace the outdated

Tylenol tampering legend as the catalyst for reexamining how we think about damage control. The Duke affair teaches us that it is possible for the purported villains to transform themselves into the victims, and that self-styled vindicators can turn out to be the true villains. The cast characters did not switch places until the accused mounted a legal and public defense that many in the academic and media communities assumed they didn't deserve.

While the Duke lacrosse case may not be the template that applies to all crises, there are lessons to be learned about how and why attack targets survive.

In the early months of the case, Durham, North Carolina District Attorney Michael Nifong, who was running for reelection, owned the primal narrative: spoiled, rich white preppies gang-raping a black woman. He referred to the accused as "a bunch of hooligans" whose "daddies could buy them expensive lawyers." On Fox's *The O'Reilly Factor,* he said "There's no doubt in my mind that she was raped . . ." As an unnamed *New York Times* alumnus said in a media exposé about the case: "You couldn't *invent* a story so precisely tuned to the outrage frequency of the modern, metropolitan, *bien-pensant* journalist."

It had all the makings of a Hollywood release: a minority rape victim (a casting director might recommend Halle Berry), obscenely privileged attackers (think the cast of *The O.C.*), a lush university setting in need of community healing (pick your elite Eastern campus), and an outraged, media-savvy DA (Tommy Lee Jones, perhaps). The Duke lacrosse coach was forced to resign and the university president cancelled the remainder of the 2006 lacrosse season. The New Black Panthers marched on Durham. Reverend Jesse Jackson echoed "something happened," and Jackson's Rainbow/PUSH Coalition promised to pay the tuition of the purported victim, Crystal Gail Mangum.

Throughout the investigation, Reade Seligmann, Collin Finnerty, and David Evans, who were widely portrayed in the press and on the Internet as out-of-control preppies, vehemently proclaimed their innocence. Said Evans before his surrender to police: "You have all been told some fantastic lies, and I look forward to watching them unravel in the weeks to come." The charges were dropped because of irrefutable evidence that the Duke players were innocent, not to mention that Mangum was catastrophically unbelievable. Her story repeatedly changed. Among other things, she initially claimed she had been raped by twenty white men. She subsequently reduced the number to the three accused. Her chronology repeatedly changed, as did her descriptions of her assailants.

An exhaustive forensic sweep by the allied defense team's investigators found evidence including time-stamped photos of the "victim" smiling in front of the alleged crime scene at the precise time when she was supposedly gang-raped, phone company records that were "triangulated" showing that Finnerty wasn't even at the location of the alleged crime, testimony of a cab driver that put Seligmann at a completely different location; time-stamped photos of Seligmann at an ATM machine at the time of the crime, and a thorough fingerprint analysis showing that one of the men had never been in the room in question. Reports surfaced that in 1996 Mangum had claimed she had been raped by three white men but she never followed through with the authorities to provide specifics.

The players' defense lawyers repeatedly approached Nifong to present exculpatory evidence and were rebuffed—the narrative locomotive had left the station. While the facts weren't on his side, the legal pundits overwhelmingly were, the talking-head programs stocking the lineup with "experts" that validated the *Animal House* idiom. Joseph Cheshire, Evans's defense attorney, said, "I came to the decision that we had to win the media war, and that if we didn't win the media war, we would be in trial." Which, given the witch-hunt climate, would have been a disaster.

Much of the defense strategy included a media campaign, which can be a very high-stakes device. Specifically, the suspects encouraged CBS's *60 Minutes* to investigate the case and even appeared on the program to defend themselves, the latter being a tactic that defense attorneys usually dismiss as being too risky. *60 Minutes,* which tends to side with victims and supposed vindicators like Nifong (and against the rich and powerful), was sympathetic to the defendants, so strong was their case.

The defense's counteroffensive surely triggered the involvement of the North Carolina State Bureau of Investigation, whose Wade Smith announced "No DNA material from any young man tested was present on the body of this complaining witness. . . . We hope with this, Mr. Nifong will announce he is not going to pursue this case further."

In April 2007, just over a year after the arrests, North Carolina Attorney General Roy Cooper dropped the charges. Cooper declared Nifong's actions a "tragic rush to accuse." Nifong was later charged and convicted of criminal contempt, disbarred, and sentenced to serve one day in prison. The families of Seligmann, Finnerty, and Evans have filed a $30 million suit against the city of Durham, Nifong, and thirteen officials associated with the case.

What are the damage control lessons of the Duke fiasco?

First and foremost, the lacrosse players had a clear and demonstrable alternative narrative (for the record, most crisis subjects don't): They were provably innocent and their accuser was not credible. Being wrongly accused, especially in a high-profile case where there is proof, is the obvious foundation of a powerful defense. The lacrosse players' counteroffensive shifted the cast characters: They had become the victims and their accuser a villain. Furthermore, the story's "vindicator"—the theoretically impartial champion of justice, DA Nifong—also was transformed into the primary villain. The new narrative byte: TOP COP GOES TO SLAMMER FOR DUKE LAX LYNCHING.

Second, the lacrosse players' families had the *will* to fight. One of the most important factors in surviving a crisis is the capacity to "go the distance" in a withering battle that has no end in sight. Many individuals and institutions talk tough at the onset of hostilities but cannot tolerate a struggle, especially one that doesn't appear to be making any progress. The Duke lacrosse's players' families, however, were properly motivated. The cost of not fighting back was disastrous—the ruined lives of promising young men.

Finally, the players had the resources and savvy to fight back. Evans' mother was a lobbyist and his father was an attorney at a blue-chip law firm. The family had lived in the nation's capital and had undoubtedly witnessed their share of Washington political witch hunts and their attendant lawyers, investigators, and media consultants. If they didn't know the damage control game themselves, they had access to those who did. Regrettably, there is often a correlation between deep pockets and the ability to defuse a crisis or attack. Attorneys, media consultants, and private investigators are expensive. Whether it's an individual or a corporation under siege, one of the first questions that should be asked before adopting a strategy is whether the necessary resources are available to fight back.

Without an aggressive, well-funded, and well-publicized counteroffensive, neither law enforcement nor the media would have revisited the initial storyline. Put differently, in the YouTube era, attack targets must do the legwork that during simpler times would have been undertaken by government authorities and the "old" media.

Despite the lacrosse players' vindications, and regardless of how they fare in their civil suit, they will spend their lives on the receiving end of whispers characterizing them as the formerly accused Duke rapists. One can never, especially with the proliferation of the Internet, neutralize all hostile voices, but Seligmann, Finnerty, and Evans are free men with bright prospects, which is why our discipline is called "damage control," not "damage disappearance."

THE CRISIS ROUNDUP

Since the original publication of *Damage Control*, there has been a veritable potpourri of crises in business, sports, entertainment, and politics. What many of these crises have in common is a base, lowest-common-denominator quality. They are fiascos that emerged not as a result of dogged journalistic exposés, but

from trafficking in voyeuristic, self-sustaining allegations on Internet blogs, late-night talk shows, and in the most tabloid of
news media. Call it the YouTube storyline—the primal narrative that everybody intuitively "gets" in a few seconds, true or
not: RIGHT-WING SENATOR SNAGGED IN GAY SEX BATHROOM
BUST; NFL STAR TORTURED PUPPIES; THOUSANDS STRANDED IN
JETBLUE "FLYING COFFINS"; CHINESE DOLLS CHOKE KIDS.

Not everyone facing crisis in recent months fared as well as
the Duke lacrosse players ultimately did. What follows is a
roundup of recent public relations fiascoes and an assessment of
how their subjects are likely to fare in the near future. An "up"
arrow means that the subject is likely to be back in business. An
"even" arrow means that the subject's situation is still in flux. A
"down" arrow means that the subject is likely to remain in crisis
and not recover any time soon from his or her original sin.

Don Imus → Shock jock called Rutgers women's basketball
team "nappy-headed hos" and lost his gig on CBS radio
and MSNBC for his racial faux pas despite a veritable road
show of apology to, among others, the Reverend Al Sharpton
who predictably didn't forgive him. The Imus case proved once
again the limits of apology as a damage control tactic. Nevertheless, he needed to apologize to the Rutgers team—and only
the Rutgers team—as the price of entry for his redemption.
Imus disappeared for six months, but at this writing, it appears
he'll reemerge in a new incarnation with ABC radio. Sometimes, the simple act of vanishing for a while is a better crisis
management technique than all of the media campaigns
Madison Avenue can conjure up. Imus is still entertaining
and controversial, which makes for great broadcasting.

Michael Vick ↓ The Atlanta Falcons quarterback pleaded guilty to charges of operating an illegal dog fighting ring, which included the torture and execution (via hanging, drowning, and electrocution) of some of these animals. Vick apologized (and found Jesus) amid incendiary public outrage, was exiled from the NFL, and lost his huge contract and blue-chip endorsements that had made him one of the biggest earners in pro sports. He still faces federal charges. Vick is headed to prison and has only one hope: Come out a humbled man who has paid his debt and pray he retains the athletic skills to make him attractive to another NFL team.

Marion Jones ↓ The Olympic track star apologized via letter to friends and family for steroid use and pleaded guilty to lying to federal agents. She has surrendered the five medals she won at the Sydney Olympics, and her once-hot endorsements have gone cold and will almost certainly never return. Her redemption can only occur not as an athlete, but by teaching a new generation that our win-at-any-cost ethic can come at a terrible price.

Senator David Vitter ↑ When Vitter (R-LA) was exposed as a patron of the notorious "DC Madam" Deborah Jean Palfrey, he copped to "a serious sin," held a news conference with his wife, and remains in office. The story died down comparatively quickly despite a renewed national debate about conservative public officials who don't practice what they preach. Vitter was not accused of a crime and his escapades were evidently heterosexual, which, political correctness notwithstanding, takes some of the sting out of his sin.

His retention of his office is a huge win, but his future clout is a question mark.

Senator Larry Craig ↓ A few months after Craig's (R-ID) arrest for soliciting sex from a male undercover police officer in an airport rest room, the story went public. Craig pleaded guilty, he claimed in a news conference, because he panicked at the arrest and had not consulted with an attorney. He said he would resign shortly. He also audaciously explained his alleged in-stall encounter by saying he had a "wide stance," which is why he tapped the police officer's feet. The news media ignited, the subtext of the outrage being that Craig, a conservative Republican, was a hypocrite who supported legislation hostile to homosexuals. Soon, Craig reversed his earlier promise to resign, and decided he would seek to have his guilty plea thrown out, remaining in the Senate pending that decision. Even when a judge upheld his guilty plea, Craig said he would stay in the Senate until the end of his term in 2009, infuriating his Republican colleagues who viewed him as radioactive. Despite his hunker down, zig-zag approach to crisis management, Craig remains in office—no small achievement—but is powerless and has entered the pantheon of sex scandals beside the J. Edgar Hoover-in-a-dress legend. Craig's only viable alternative would have been to fight the charges from the outset. This, however, would not have averted torrential media scrutiny and may, in fact, have made the scandal even worse with day-by-day updates in his case. The senator had no good options.

JetBlue ↑ Low-cost airliner JetBlue apologized to customers for canceling 1,100 flights during a February 2007 snowstorm, which stranded thousands of passengers in snow-covered airplanes (an irate passenger described it as like being trapped in a coffin) on airport runways for as much as ten hours. JetBlue reimbursed customers and issued a passengers' "Bill of Rights," which "spells out the specific compensation, in the form of electronic travel vouchers, that our customers will receive if they are inconvenienced due to a delay or cancellation that is within JetBlue's control." CEO David Neeleman, who deftly handled a hostile media, nevertheless stepped down a few months after the fiasco, a testament that in a crisis nothing is more powerful than the need to blame somebody. The stock, at this writing, is down from its January 2007 high, but stabilizing. JetBlue is wrestling with the consequences of having grown too quickly, but some analysts are bullish on the company's potential performance in 2008.

Mattel ↑ The toy manufacturer initiated a series of voluntary recalls after some of its products manufactured in China were deemed unsafe by consumer groups and regulators. CEO Bob Eckert apologized at a congressional hearing and posted a videotaped message to consumers on Mattel's Web site promising to identify potential product faults, ranging from small parts that could pose choking hazards to lead paint that children could swallow, and fix them. The company did the right thing, which set the foundation for a recovery in the long-term.

China → After a ham-fisted start blaming American product designs versus its own manufacturing practices, China has started to realize that if the country is to compete in the long-term, its leaders have to bring its safety standards into the twenty-first century. This is a multiyear proposition and the Chinese government cannot institute huge systemic changes overnight.

Alberto Gonzales ↓ After months of hunkering down amid reports of a campaign by the Department of Justice to fire politically uncooperative U.S. attorneys, the White House accepted the resignation of Attorney General Gonzales. During blistering congressional hearings, Gonzales appeared overwhelmed. His answers struck many as the kind one might expect from a low-level bureaucrat, not America's sheriff. In a climate where accusations of lying have become a core part of the anti-Bush narrative, Gonzales's damage control approach didn't work. He'll do fine in private practice, but his tenure will be forever tinged with disgrace. Could Gonzales have handled the scandal better once it broke? Conventional wisdom suggests that greater candor might have earned him a pass from Congress, but we doubt it. Such disclosure would have almost certainly required Gonzales to admit to forcing out targeted U.S. attorneys for political reasons. Such an admission would have swiftly led to his ouster. Perhaps Gonzales's only other option would have been to step down earlier in the process in order to avoid the damage to his reputation that resulted from the hearings.

Bush on the Iraq War ↓ Americans don't like wars, we like war movies—fast, decisive, and the good guys don't get hurt. No weapons of mass destruction were found in Iraq, the ostensible goal of the war, and while Saddam was neutralized, there is no stable new regime. There is a bloody civil war and a seemingly never-ending stream of casualties, which, in contemporary public opinion means somebody botched the job. World opinion is heavily antiwar. The math on wartime communications is simple: when you're winning a war, you get "good PR"; when you're losing you don't. Contrary to our culture's spin-worship, slick communications programs are not the antidote to terrible real-world events. The first rule of effective damage control is having a realistic appreciation of what important audiences can stomach. The Bush team's plan was anchored in utopian notions that Americans would be willing to make the sacrifices necessary to bring democracy to Iraq (we weren't) and that Iraqis would appreciate the United States as liberators. It's hard to be grateful, at least in the short term, when your country erupts into civil war. If history vindicates Bush, that vindication is many years away.

Bill Belichick ↑ The brilliant New England Patriots coach apologized for "misinterpreting" NFL rules amid accusations that he authorized the videotaping of the strategy signals of opposing teams, including during a Super Bowl game. He paid a $500,000 fine while denying that he had actually used the videos to gain an advantage in games. Despite the requisite cries for him to fess up, Belichick didn't comment beyond his craftily worded I'm-not-really-sorry "apology." And he may just have been right. The NFL destroyed the telltale tapes, which guaranteed, among other things, they will never appear on YouTube.

Healthcare Industry → While Michael Moore's film *Sicko* didn't have the shock value of his earlier anti-Bush screed *Fahrenheit 911*, it received widespread media attention and reinforced the twin hot buttons that spell trouble for U.S. healthcare providers and drug companies: how such an affluent country can have so many uninsured citizens and the exorbitant cost of doctors and drugs. The healthcare industry has largely been in hunker down mode in response to *Sicko,* recognizing that one doesn't win "debates" against demagogues—especially those who moderates agree with on this issue. While some industry groups criticized the film, think tanks and politicians did most of the anti-Moore heavy lifting. The anti-healthcare industry sentiment is so venomous that even the most assertive communications campaign will not be an antidote to a deeply entrenched and broadly supported reform apparatus.

Hillary Clinton ↑ Clinton's capacity to weather blistering portrayals of her as being a cold, greedy, left-wing, Machiavellian schemer over a sixteen year period is paying off. Clinton has been so savagely demonized that the public is beginning to discover a contrast that would have been unheard of a few short years ago: She has been an able legislator with a gift for soberly articulating views on meaningful issues. Clinton has effectively tacked to the political center and, to the horror of Republicans, is capable of alternatively conveying vulnerability, humanity and, most importantly, resilience. The conservative crusade against Clinton worked in the 1990s, but may end up backfiring in the following decade, fulfilling her dream of being the first woman, and second Clinton, in the Oval Office.

RICHARD JEWELL'S DAMAGE CONTROL LEGACY

It is appropriate to conclude by observing the death of falsely accused Atlanta Olympic bomber on August 29, 2007 of heart disease and diabetes. The 1996 bombing killed one woman and injured one hundred (a cameraman died of a heart attack while covering the explosion). Jewell was forty-four. Elusive bomber Eric Robert Rudolph was arrested and convicted of this crime and abortion clinic bombings after years at large. Jewell was later lauded as a hero who saved lives by clearing the crowd away from the bomb when he spotted the suspicious backpack.

Jewell eventually reached financial settlements with the *New York Post* and NBC for suggesting he was the bomber. His case against the *Atlanta Journal Constitution* was pending at the time of his death.

Jewell's legacy is a stark reminder that individuals and institutions are increasingly vulnerable to the caprice of a culture that thrives on primal narratives and their complicit technologies. Jewell taught us why muscular counteroffensives merit a page or two in one's damage control playbook.

CHAPTER 20

Our Permanent Leakocracy

There have always been turncoats, spies, and leaks. But never has betrayal come in such torrential volume—a virulent and global distribution system—with such incentives and so few consequences. The rise of Julian Assange's WikiLeaks, an online international receptacle and merchandizing system for unauthorized information, comes to us sprinkled with the holy water of "transparency" and represents a risk to capitalism on par with the current Great Recession. From the perspective of corporate crisis management, that's a bad thing.

WikiLeaks's biggest target to date has been the U.S. military, the portal being the recipient of "the largest military security breaches in history" with its documents on the Afghanistan and Iraq wars, according to *Forbes*. WikiLeaks disclosed the names of Afghans cited as informants or employees of U.S. troops. Assange said they behaved in a criminal way and told the *Times* of London that if something happened to them as a result, it represented collateral damage from his campaign for truth.

WikiLeaks is not an equal opportunity offender; it has become an ideological enterprise that goes after "establishment" targets such as military and corporate institutions. At the time of this writing, Assange has said his next targets will be corporations. He estimates that half the documents he has yet to release from his arsenal relate to companies. Assange, a computer hacker by training, has pled guilty to twenty-four charges of illegal computer infiltration. He is a founder of a hacking fraternity known as the International Subversives. How one feels about the emergence of WikiLeaks depends a lot on one's likelihood of being targeted by the portal. As Assange said himself when asked about his modus operandi: "Pain for the guilty." So if you work for a corporation, consider yourself convicted.

WikiLeaks's supporters are vindictive and capable of causing businesses damage, although this "pain" is still to be quantified. At the end of 2010, "Operation Payback" was announced —digital attacks performed by a scattered group of Internet hackers to punish businesses that refuse to host WikiLeaks. In one undisclosed online chat room, members of Operation Payback posted the fax numbers of half a dozen corporations; it called on volunteers to fill these fax machines with unsolicited messages, using such free online fax services as MyFax.com and FaxZero.com. When accessing corporate sites, volunteers were asked to use "anonymizing" software (such as the Tor Project) to avoid being tracked by authorities.

Transparency anyone? Imagine what would happen if a corporate or government target, hiding behind the cloak of anonymity, commenced an organized program of "payback"? (We know, but we're good people going after *bad* people. . . .)

A GUARANTEED FORUM

Even prior to WikiLeaks, the Internet has presented a problem for corporations that seek discretion. There are a few reasons for this. For one thing, leaking used to be hard. The leaker had to first endure the anxiety associated with betraying his employer. He then had to obtain the telltale document, often a risky proposition in and of itself. Then he had to arrange for its duplication and distribution, which required the conspicuous acts of operating a photocopier and fraudulently encoding project numbers, then smuggle a fat envelope out of his workplace and deliver it to the intended media outlet—another potential point of exposure. These days, all a leaker has to do is sweep telltale documents onto a Zip drive or push the send button on a keyboard. Under normal circumstances, leakers can be tracked through an Internet provider address; but in the hands of world-renowned hackers, anonymity can be assured.

Another reason why leaking has become easier is the virtual certainty that one's leak will be publicized in a forum that embarrasses the target—WikiLeaks or someplace less notorious. In years past, there was always a good chance that a more prestigious media outlet would reject the material as being unworthy of airing, if it even found its way to a decision maker. Today, however, prestige media can traffic in cyberleaks under the guise of reporting on a technological phenomenon, or they can appear to be covering the reaction or fallout to the leak. This results in even more viewers stampeding to the leak-originating website.

All this is aggravated by a legal system that offers incentives to self-styled whistleblowers that would make a Wall Street investment banker blush. In a recent case, one whistleblower personally received $96 million for alleging misdeeds at a major pharmaceutical company. Such jackpots motivate the aggrieved to seek valuable cash prizes rather than work from within the business to fix problems. It also enables malfeasance by fostering the creation of documents that will have marquee value to WikiLeaks. This dynamic makes whistleblowing an exercise in self-enrichment, not public service.

And cash rewards aren't the only dubious motivation behind whistleblowing. Sometimes it is notoriety. In late 2010, a Sacramento, California, airline pilot virally broadcast a video showing lapses in his small airline's security rather than go to the proper authorities. He succeeded only in alerting would-be terrorists to how to become more effective purveyors of mayhem. As the Heisenberg effect teaches in physics, atoms behave differently when being observed. Would-be WikiLeaks stars will be tempted to choreograph corporate skullduggery in order to yield maximum damage to the target, versus maximum public good.

IS TRANSPARENCY ALWAYS GOOD?

The term *transparency* has become the shibboleth of virtue these days. No one would dispute that greater disclosure in certain areas can serve an essential purpose, namely keeping large institutions honest when the public's welfare is at stake. In an open society, we should be able to know where our tax dollars are going or what previously undisclosed studies tell us about the safety of medications. But there are also legitimate reasons to preserve confidentiality. Corporations genuinely *do* want to keep trade secrets from their competitors. And it is essential for the military to prevent its enemies from knowing where it might strike and what strategy it might use. WikiLeaks's 2010 revelation of secret U.S. diplomatic cables fell far short of having the effect of the Pentagon Papers, the twentieth-century uberleak that taught the public something new. The upshot of the Pentagon Papers was that American leaders' actions in Vietnam were sharply different from what the public was told. It was a case of secrecy run amok versus WikiLeaks's State Department cables, which amounted to little more than harmful ad hominem gossip.

Why shouldn't such cables be released? Because it is crucial to our national interests that U.S. diplomats be able to share their candid assessments of our partners and adversaries without having their blunt and intimate comments end up in the *New York Times*. Of course, Assange knows this, which is why it is clear that he has already chosen sides and seeks to use his embarrassing disclosures as weapons in a one-man policy war.

WikiLeaks's leaders understand the value of secrecy better than they let on. It remains a mystery who is on its board of directors, where it gets its funding, and the nature of its relationship with its sources; for example, does WikiLeaks actively finance and illegally conspire to obtain secret information?

Assange has also expressed indignation over—get this— leaks about his own sexual assault charges making their way through U.K. courts. When asked about the charges, he either condemns the leaks or storms off camera. The message: Assange believes in the squirming transparency of others (bad people) but not himself (good people), which validates the idea that WikiLeaks is anchored in a specific agenda, not a noble principle. When good people are discreet, it's called privacy. When bad people are discreet, it's called secrecy.

The "I am moral; you are not" construct is not limited to WikiLeaks. Many corporate detractors operate on a self-selecting "ends justify the means" system rather than a principle of universal transparency. It is acceptable to use the most invasive techniques available, including the solicitation of illegally acquired internal documents, to gather damaging information about corporate targets. But the mere suggestion that corporate critics are in need of scrutiny has the whiff of dirty tricks, and businesses are well advised to recognize the perils of such an endeavor.

The public, for example, would be astounded to learn about the huge role plaintiffs' lawyers play in quietly funding organizations that peddle health scares, not to mention the mainstream media's reliance on this confederacy for their "news" stories. Don't expect an exposé on this subject anytime soon, because the media won't touch it, and no sane corporate interest would conduct the kind of research necessary to bring this phenomenon to light.

There is also the pesky matter of ideology and fairness: Will WikiLeaks be as passionate in its solicitation of exculpatory information about its targets as it will be in its prosecution? Will the consumer public and mainstream media have any interest in vindication? Decades of frontline experience in crisis management strongly suggest not: It is a lot easier to destroy a prominent target than it is to vindicate one. There is neither media nor public interest in vindication.

IS THERE AN ANTIDOTE TO WIKILEAKS?

Businesses and individuals are searching for an algorithm for managing the risks associated with WikiLeaks. This will prove to be a daunting challenge. For one thing, much of WikiLeaks's activities are protected by law. Existing free-expression laws combined with the near impossibility of affirmatively linking leaked documents with particular jurisdictions—electronic data zips around the world at lightning speed—render online leak portals essentially immune from legal attack. An even more troubling obstacle, perhaps, is WikiLeaks's popularity among large segments of the public. Assange was named the readers' choice for *Time* magazine's Person of the Year in 2010, and blogging traffic is substantially pro-WikiLeaks.

There are defensive exercises, however, to help manage the threat posed by WikiLeaks and similar portals:

1. **Inoculate against charges of unethical behavior**

   During the past decade, there has been an explosion in the number, type, and reach of laws and regulations governing corporate behavior. This is especially true for companies that do business with the federal government and/or foreign nations. Make sure all managers are adequately trained and educated in these mandates. Establish clear corporate policies that will help ensure compliance.

2.   Differentiate between good and bad leakers

To the extent there will be any success at all in combating WikiLeaks, it will be on the front end, before publication, by differentiating between people who are trying to do the right thing and those motivated purely by self-interest. Confidentiality agreements may be dissuasive if they explicitly state that legal redress will be sought in cases where someone leaks information without having made earnest efforts to correct problems through existing channels. To this end, companies must establish their own whistleblower reporting mechanisms and ensure confidentiality and protection for people who go to the company first. Establishing the rules of play *before* leaks occur is more effective than seeking redress on the publication end, which will likely remain protected.

There are greater legal criminal and civil risks for someone who betrays government or corporate secrets than there are for media or Internet venues, which will plausibly argue that they were passive recipients of documents. To cover himself legally, Assange has preposterously claimed that WikiLeaks does not encourage leaking, which is akin to a bank claiming it discourages deposits. As of this writing, the Department of Justice is pursuing charges against Assange and U.S. Army intelligence analyst Bradley Manning, who leaked tens of thousands of documents to Assange. In this affair Assange is vulnerable, in theory, for allegedly soliciting the documents and engineering their receipt, not publishing them.

Corporations must weigh the risks and benefits of seeking actionable confidentiality agreements with employees and consultants upon employment and engagement where all parties are clear on the penalties. Such agreements and their enforcement will dissuade some, but not all breaches.

3. **Vulnerability assessment and preparation**

What are you worried about at three in the morning?

This is the question we often ask clients when they want to know what their greatest vulnerabilities are. Brainstorming about every conceivable leak scenario is not constructive, but identifying a few areas of vulnerability and scouring existing "leakable" documentation attendant to these areas can be a valuable exercise. Say you work for a pharmaceutical company that manufactures a blockbuster drug. Any successful drug is associated with extensive correspondence and analysis. Included in this trove of information will be vigorous debate, including an assessment of side effects, that can easily be taken out of context and made to appear sinister ("You *knew* about this side effect and still put the drug on the market?"). Knowing there is a 100 percent chance that such data exists in corporate records, identify the troubling narratives in advance of a leak and prepare to characterize them for public consumption. Assume they will be made public and deliberately taken out of context.

4. Create your own Information portal

Once areas of vulnerability have been established, create a "dark" website (one that is not yet being broadcast live) that contains a counternarrative answering the allegations likely to be made. This website can include interviews with key players and spokespersons who can contextualize the subject at hand. If the leaks are actually made public, social media—Facebook, Twitter, targeted blogs—can be leveraged to publicize the newly "live" website.

5. Technological firewalls

Predictably, there is no shortage of tech gurus peddling software and other discretion elixirs. On December 20, 2010, Toshiba American Business Solutions (TABS) announced it will host an educational webinar on securing against a WikiLeaks–type data breach. Electronic defense mechanisms include firewall protection (preventing hacking by hostile parties) and keyword searching and "packet sniffing" (whereby certain sensitive terms are flagged when documents containing them are compromised). The challenge with the latter techniques is that they can be overly invasive, not to mention yielding many false breach positives. The work in this area is in its infancy so it is hard to assess its real-world value, but new technologies will surely be an important part of the security mosaic.

6. Management firewalls

Despite the best efforts of corporations to institutional-ize discretion, we have found it to be an exercise in futility. The corporate mentality is such that many executives oper-ate under the delusion that those who work for the company are on the "same team." The reality is that very few leaks come from external hackers; an overwhelming majority originate with trusted internal team members and consultants*. The only people who understand electronic discretion are those who have paid a steep price in terms of personal exposure or costly legal fees. This accounts for a tiny percentage of the population. Nevertheless, smart companies are increasingly forming special teams to man-age sensitive issues. Intimate, subject-specific teams—as op-posed to porous, "democratic" committees—tend to be more discreet about communications and perceive greater risk of punishment.

7. Pool resources

Targets of WikiLeaks have begun to, at least informally, coalesce around possible approaches to fighting back. Shortly before this writing, Bank of America, MasterCard, Visa, Apple, and PayPal, one by one, refused to provide ser-vices to WikiLeaks. It is uncertain how WikiLeaks's desire to

* Conventional public relations firms are especially porous with information. Very few have confidentiality agree-ments with clients and, even if they do, the individuals who work for these firms have been inculcated in a culture of information sharing. They also often have longstanding loyalties to journalists and nongovernmental organizations that supersede perceived loyalties to ephemeral clients.

receive services from the same corporations it attacks will play out. After all, mainstream media organizations have consistently enjoyed robust advertising from the same corporations their journalists investigate. In these early stages, an exchange of information among WikiLeaks's targets merits continued exploration.

FOREVER LEAKY

Regardless of Assange's fate, massive informational leaks are a permanent part of our landscape—with a twist: the seemingly powerless guerilla Davids of WikiLeaks fighting the Goliaths of industry will be proven to be, in fact, the Goliaths on the Internet battlefield. In all likelihood, others shrewder, subtler, and without Assange's baggage will come along with a more lasting portals. Former WikiLeaks employee Daniel Domscheit-Berg, for example, has broken off from WikiLeaks and is starting another outfit, OpenLeaks.

Aware of both the public demand for the mortification of our institutions and leaders and the laws that encourage informational breaches, these portals will play a major role in shaping behavior, for better or for worse. Corporations would be well advised to accept the permanence of this state of play and take discrete actions to both accommodate and resist it, as their interests dictate. The bad news, of course, is the limited control we have over WikiLeaks and its descendants. The good news is that steps can be taken to hedge against this viral trend and the reality that the volume of these leaks will be so enormous that today's leak may be tomorrow's background noise.

INDEX